CASA
MEXI
CANA

CASA
MEXI
CANA

TEXT AND PHOTOGRAPHS BY
TIM STREET-PORTER

■

INTRODUCTION BY
MARIE-PIERRE COLLE

STEWART, TABORI & CHANG

NEW YORK

Introduction translated by Kenneth L. Krabbenhoft

Originally published in English hardcover in 1989

Paperback edition published in 1994 by
Stewart, Tabori & Chang
115 West 18th Street
New York, NY 10011

Canadian Distribution:
Canadian Manda Group
One Atlantic Avenue, Suite 105
Toronto, Ontario M6K 3E7
Canada

Library of Congress Cataloging-in-Publication Data
Street-Porter, Tim.
    Casa Mexicana: the architecture, design, and style of Mexico / text and photographs by Tim Street-Porter : introduction by Marie-Pierre Cole.
        p. cm
    Includes index.
    ISBN: 1-55670-097-0 (hardcover)
    ISBN: 1-55670-367-8 (paperback)
    1. Architecture, Domestic—Mexico. 2. Interior decoration—Mexico. I. Title.
    NA7244.S77   1989   89-11382
    728'.37'0972—dc20   CIP

Printed in Japan

10 9 8

Stewart, Tabori & Chang is a subsidiary of

LA MARTINIÈRE
GROUPE

PAGE 2: Barragán's signature cluster of *pulque* pots decorates a patio outside the sitting room of Casa Gilardi. The wall is high enough to shut out the city; the blue is a metaphor for the sky. ABOVE, LEFT TO RIGHT: Staircase to the guest rooms of Casa Ortiz Monasterio. Façade of a country cottage near Querétaro. A collection of Mexican masks in the living room of Olga and Rufino Tamayo. A blue tower against a blue sky in Careyes. A corner table and collection of artifacts, all from Mexico, in Anne Kelly's Los Angeles house. A romantic linking of the owners' names in the kitchen of the Cortina residence. A traditionally decorated side table. An upper-level promenade at the hacienda of Tenango.

CONTENTS

THE MEXICAN HOUSE

The sky is the true façade of a house.
Luis Barragán

T he grace of imperfection is worth more than grace-less perfection," says architect and anthropologist Alex von Wuthenau. Mexican style is grace itself. Its perfection lies in the unexpected, a quality André Breton called surrealistic. Our reality is a cross between light and shadow, tears and laughter, life and death, truth and fantasy, innocence and wisdom. It embraces the way we live and the sense we make of life. Because it is so complex and unsettling, Mexican reality must be understood intuitively, through the senses. In this way alone can we grasp the essence of what is Mexican.

Variety is the spice of this land. We range across limitless expanses, and amazement turns commonplace as we move from desert to seashore, from jungle to mountaintop, from a capital with twenty million inhabitants to wilderness where time seems to stand still.

Varied as it is, the geography of Mexico has a distinguishing mark, a harshness. Almost every vista ends in a mountain range. The environment makes itself felt, and man translates its grandeur into the

OPPOSITE: A harmonious blending of the colors of nature with painted surfaces in the courtyard of architect Marco Aldaco's own recently finished house in Guadalajara.

Above: This tiny, primitive chapel at Oxtotipac, built in the sixteenth century by Franciscan monks, speaks eloquently of "the grace of imperfection." RIGHT: An arrangement of fruit in the dining room of Casa Galvez; the painting behind is by Pedro Coronel. BELOW RIGHT: Mexico is famous for its walls of vivid colors and rich patinas. FAR RIGHT: A field of agave near the town of Tequila in Jalisco.

BELOW: A shocking-pink Virgin from Metepec occupies a niche outside a family chapel. BOTTOM: The front door of a cottage near Querétaro.

LEFT: Accidental color relationships enliven a street on the outskirts of Puebla. BELOW: An attractively varicolored tiled roof in Acapulco. BOTTOM: The Pyramid of the Feathered Serpents, Xochicalco.

human scale by building in harmony with what surrounds him—desert, high plains, and jungle interpreted in roof lines, walls, and windows.

Nature is a quarry from which we extract raw materials, present even when transformed by human hands. Chiluca stone and tezontle—always an echo of the Sierras—were as much a part of pre-Columbian buildings as they are of ours today. The volcanoes are here in the walls.

Although the peasant's house begins as the color of the Mexican earth, when it comes time to decorate, the outside is painted to enrich it. Color is the essence of the Mexican spirit, the one luxury in a poor man's home. We see it in fabrics, in *huipiles* (women's sleeveless shirts), in the fruits of the marketplace. It has been an element of popular architecture from the polychromed pyramids to the baroque churches of the colony to today's modern homes.

The Mexican land, which gave birth to the Toltecs and the Mayas, has felt the impact of many invasions—the Spaniards of Cortés, the French of Maximilian, and the Americans of General Scott. Over time it has become a mosaic, and each piece has a story to tell. A Mexican building, like a chorus of voices, sings a hymn of its heritage. Thus the hieratic, almost oriental silence of a pyramid is as much ours as a noisy celebration in the atrium of a baroque church, and the city's fast-moving jumble of forms complements the quiet presence of a *palapa* at the edge of the Pacific Ocean.

Mexican style is a harvest of these elements sown by time and history. It exists in open spaces and enclosed courtyards, in the use of contrast, and in myriad small details like grillwork, column supports, and stairs. It is in the texture of woven palm rugs, in roofing shakes and tawny tepetate stone, in *equipales* (rough-hewn chairs of pigskin and wood), in the painted trim of statuary niches and earthenware pots.

The Mexican house, a place of privacy and individual expression, is also where the Mexican relates to his family, friends, and the world at large. The kitchen and a well-set table are important, but so are intimate corners where he can be alone.

Jealous of his solitude, the Mexican takes refuge in his house. The walls protect him, holding the world at bay. He likes to live in a space that speaks of stability, safety, and permanence. This sense of belonging to the house, this connection with a time and place that relates life to death and presence to absence is of utmost importance.

The Mexican house strives to be a creative statement, a context for the expression of a unique and inimitable lifestyle, its symbols and customs. The house—that part of us which opens its arms, smiles, beckons, and welcomes—is alive with details that always speak of the past.

The warm colors of the façade extend a welcome. In Puebla, for example, they symbolized wealth and prestige. Walls are faced in earthenware tiles interspersed with ceramic mosaics. Doors and windows wear wreaths of sculpted plaster and mortar to which wrought iron grillwork, railings, and gargoyles are added. The occasional floral niche transforms an outside corner into a ship's prow with a patron saint for a figurehead.

The courtyard is at the center of the house, an arrangement made possible—perhaps necessitated—by a mild year-round climate. It is outside, but it is also a part of what is inside the house. Mexicans have always favored enclosed spaces, be it the entrance to the inner sanctum of an ancient temple, the walled plaza surrounding a pyramid, or later, the monastic cloister. Mexicans live within themselves, defining the relationship between outdoors and indoors so as to ensure their privacy. Thus the courtyard of a Mexican's house reflects a complex heritage shared by Andalusian grandparents, Moorish great-grandparents, and great-great grandparents who were Mayan or Teotihuacán.

These houses are full of objects that reflect a very Mexican zeal to inhabit space, to impart a sense of baroque fullness. Modern architects take us away from this penchant for excess. They create silences and gaps that recall the speechlessness of pre-Columbian architecture, offering spaces in which to relax, breathe deeply, and feel the changes of the seasons.

Each house has its own man-made emotional climate, a pleasing

Interesting patterns on tiled façades in Puebla, which was Mexico's tile-producing center. Puebla is famous for its decorated façades and wall surfaces.

14

Texture and color combine in this street scene in Michoacán.

combination of texture and color. More than ornament, this climate is a unifying force, an effect that can expand or contract, warm or cool a space. It is essential to Mexican architecture, which attempts to create an emotional response.

Architecture bears the imprint of cultural evolution. In Mexico it follows two paths, one rural, the other urban. The isolation of the rural environment has produced a timeless vernacular architecture that uses local materials and hardly needs architects. Its creations reflect popular culture. The coastal village, with its *palapas* roofed in palm fronds, its fences made out of sticks, its wood and adobe speaking of the closeness of the earth—it has not changed since pre-Columbian times. The cabañas of Michoacán have seen years of rain fall in front of their hewn-log doorways, while the adobe houses of the altiplano village have held the often blinding sun at bay behind walls that are often whitewashed, with a red dado along the bottom.

The beaches of the Pacific and the Caribbean have an extravagant natural beauty. For some of today's architects they are a source of inspiration, a place where they can dream and give free rein to their imaginations. They build houses to become part of the natural setting, mimicking the coastline with round swimming pools and jacuzzis. They build *palapas* rounded like the trunks of native cayaco palms wrapped in the strangling embrace of climbing amates. (The thatch is woven of royal palm fronds cut and treated by the full moon, when their sap is most abundant.) The dining table and *equipales* are round, and handmade pots from Oaxaca have fat round bellies. Everything is sensual.

There are no doors. Openings are cut in walls that bend and shrink or unfold, transformed into benches, chairs, balustrades, screens. The wall may be ochre, washed-out pink, or faded orange; it may have a yellow edging. Angles disappear, edges grow smoother. The wall foreshortens, perhaps, creating a niche or a window to frame a lordly agave.

A re-creation of the sacred *cenotes* (sunken sacrificial pools) at Chichén Itzá, this modern swimming pool is enclosed by artificial rocks.

his is where and how we find our roots. The craftsman transforms and translates his landscape, creating something distinctively his own. Under the colonial Viceroys, such craftsmen gave new and often surprising expression to old Spanish forms.

The center of civil life in the countryside was the hacienda: an independent, self-sufficient, essentially feudal world where everyone worked and lived together under the guidance of the hacienda's owner. These communities took the place of the native chiefdoms and beginning in the time of Cortés received formal recognition as land-grants. What we now know as the colonial style came into being in the shadow of the hacienda's granaries, where attachment to the earth and the rituals of labor helped define the character of Mexican life forever. Huge *trojes* (sheds for storing grain), work areas, a chapel— all were key elements in the raising of wheat, cattle, sugar, or cactus for brewing the alcoholic drink called *pulque*. Each hacienda was the miniature capital of a territory often too vast for the eye to take in at a glance.

In the cities it was different. Closer to civilization, people lived by trading. The colonial city's pre-Columbian antecedents were grounded in an essentially religious function. They served as places to commune with the universe or connect with the landscape of earth and sky. Each culture created new forms: the Zapotecs built Monte Albán in order to reach the sky; the monumental scale of a Teotihuacán structure made it "a place where men become gods." In the jungle at Palenque the Mayans fashioned an altar for the study of the stars, while the greatness of the Aztecs is evident in the Templo Mayor, which is a summation of their culture and their wisdom. In all of these buildings we detect a universe that is far closer to the emotions than to logic.

The Spanish conquest imposed European notions on Mexican tradition. While the spirit of the Renaissance made itself felt in the planning of new cities, local geographic and technological conditions determined that the pre-Columbian character of the Mexican city asserted itself as well. With colors, for example, Mexico City's

Top: Monte Albán is one of the most spectacular sites in Mesoamerica. Built on a lofty hilltop above a broad valley, it is surrounded by distant hills and clouds. BOTTOM: The kitchen of the former convent of Santa Rosa in Puebla, where *mole poblano* was invented. Walls, ceiling, and floor are covered in small, glazed tiles.

A pretty, sun-splashed fountain built into the wall behind the cathedral in San Miguel de Allende.

tones reflect the combination of tezontle's volcanic red and gray masonry; in Morelia, rose-colored stone; in Zacatecas, gold; and green in Oaxaca.

The colonial building is a mixture of cultures decorated by the lavish, uninhibited imagination with which the indigenous hand embellished Spanish forms. The colonial house, though, follows a plan that leaves little room for experimentation. The entranceway is broad so that carriages can get through. To one side is the porter's lodge; to the other, the warehouse. The ground floor, with its wide roof, encircles the courtyard—the focal point of the workday. The upper floor, with its halls and railings, birdcages and plants, is for residential use; it bears the stamp of a quiet, provincial life.

While foreign influences have always passed through the filter of local idiosyncrasies, there were times when imitation displaced invention. The emulation of things French during Emperor Maximilian's reign replaced Spanish sobriety with a taste for neoclassicism and palatial architecture. Terraces were appended to Chapultepec Palace, and, for the first time, attention was paid to gardens, statuary, and sidewalks. Under the presidency of Porfirio Díaz, Mexican cities strove to imitate Paris; only in the countryside were the flavors of adobe, whitewash, and roofing tiles preserved.

Between 1920 and 1950 the Mexican city was modernized, at first building along lines laid down by the past, then throwing itself into new styles, anxious to catch up with the international avant-garde. As elsewhere, this movement gave way to the symmetries of Art Deco, examples of which can be found from Chihuahua to Mérida. This spurt of innovation created a demand for forward-looking architects. Functionalism became the rage, and the Bauhaus made its entrance. Later, architects José Villagrán and Vladimir Kaspe introduced Le Corbusier, and skyscrapers were built in imitation of those in the United States. Rectangles and glass soon dominated the landscape.

At the same time, a nationalistic movement came into being, and interior decoration began to look at native Mexican style. The painter

TOP: Outdoing Hollywood. During the 1930s the nouveau riche in Mexico City built ostentatious houses in a style re-imported from Los Angeles. These houses are affectionately called Hollywood Spanish. BOTTOM: The art-deco style proved very popular in Mexico City in the 1930s. This stylish window grille is in the Colonia Roma.

and decorator Chucho Reyes established a dialogue between turn-of-the-century urbanism and popular Mexican taste. Reyes proposed creating spaces out of dreams and the imagination, using colors that reveal the light of the sun at dawn or nighttime reflections.

Reyes reminded us that the colors of the marketplace—sweets and fruits and toys—are all part of the environment. He invited us to live with them, to participate in "the adventure of disorder," to enjoy the feeling of popular art and the magic of color.

Walls in his house resemble altars crowded with souvenirs, paintings of saints, decorative plates, portraits in oil, and drawings on colored wrapping paper. Alongside candles and mirrors are colored-glass globes of the kind that were found in turn-of-the-century *pulque* bars. In his house, light is meted out in doses, color brightening and intensifying the atmosphere of the rooms. He used square panes of glass painted yellow to create other sources of light: they flood the place with sunlight reduced to its simplest expression. It is this idea that Barragán used years later in the Tlalpan Chapel and in the Gilardi house in Tacubaya.

Luis Barragán is the most distinguished architect that contemporary Mexico has produced. Indeed, the Mexican style in modern architecture began with him. He gave universal form to concepts explored together with Reyes, endowing them with the kind of presence that transforms mere spaces into dynamic elements of living environments.

Chucho and Luis were friends. They were both from Guadalajara, and they worked together. Barragán sought Reyes's advice and painted his buildings with colors from Reyes's paintings. Barragán took Reyes's wood-and-parchment chair, after a Philippine design, and made it a fixture in modern houses. They say it was Chucho Reyes who demonstrated to Barragán the proportions of the staircase Barragán made famous in his own house by folding a napkin into an accordion shape one day when they were eating lunch in a restaurant.

Luis Barragán inaugurated a new era in Mexican architecture. Each project became a world in itself, with specific problems to be solved. Barragán created a spare, enriching language in which each element was specially chosen to evoke an aspect of the Mexican's relationship

OPPOSITE TOP: A rare angel sconce by Chucho Reyes in the residence of architect Enrique del Moral. BOTTOM: *Pulque* pots from Michoacán grouped on the front patio of the house Barragán built for the Galvez family. ABOVE: The entry porch of one of Barragán's first houses (Guadalajara, 1930), showing a North African-Moorish influence.

to life. His achievements changed forever our way of conceptualizing space. They taught us that functionalism is not the only way and obliged us to search for our roots.

Barragán's ideals were mysticism, beauty, silence, solitude. "I believe in an emotional architecture. It is important that mankind be moved by architectural beauty. If there are a number of equally valid technical solutions to a problem, the one that delivers a message of beauty and emotion to the inhabitant—that one is true architecture." He also believed in color, and when asked why color was such a dominant element in his buildings, replied, "For the sheer pleasure of using and enjoying it."

Barragán's creations combine the secrecy of Moorish courtyards with the silence of the convent, surrounded by walls that shelter and protect. They have been compared to set designs. "Why not?," said Barragán, "scenery for the theater of life."

Natural materials, traditional materials—these are used to impart warmth to the impersonality of contemporary style. The key, it seems, is to create spaces in accordance with an almost religious devotion to intimacy. Benches, single-panel or folding screens, walls that do double duty as furniture and weight-bearing partitions: all reach beyond their practical function of providing support and protection, to embrace open space. In this architecture of simplicity, color is a piece of glory, clothing for a wall that connects it with its surroundings.

Imaginative design cannot become reality without the fine workmanship of Mexico's masons, carpenters, and blacksmiths, who have mastered the techniques that link today's architecture with that of the country's past. And today's architects offer a variety of challenges to these craftsmen. Some architects continue the tradition of Barragán and deal with questions of shape, volume, and color. Others look to the landscape; others still, to colonial traditions and the belief that protective walls and high ceilings are necessary elements. And in their institutional buildings, a group of contemporary architects show the majestic scale of pre-Hispanic Mexico adapted to the needs of today.

Opposite: The "red patio" at the end of the back garden of Barragán's Casa Galvez is covered with red terra-cotta paving. The family meets here for family picnics. The back wall is part of a theater owned by the Galvez family.

Opposite: The dining room of the hacienda of San Juan Tlacapecpan, with color and decoration reminiscent of Frida Kahlo's house. The frescoed borders, painted by a local Indian artist, are copied from sixteenth-century originals. The fruit bowl is painted, but the lacquered wood fruit are glued onto the wall. Below this is a display of ceramics and an ornate Mexican hope chest.

But all exhibit their love of Mexico, a land of madness huge enough to embrace anything—past, present, and future.

To experience fine architecture is like entering a dining room—the place that awakens our appetite—or a bedroom that invites us to take a siesta or a sitting room where a party is going on. We delight in the proportions and colors of these spaces, and the way they capture sunlight. Beauty exists or it does not. One can reach it only by accepting the one rule that matters, the rule that says there are no rules.

A door is opening before us. It welcomes us to come in and look around. It is the pride of fine hospitality, which offers us peace and the love of life. Inside, the Virgin of Guadalupe comes forward to welcome us and, so it seems, to give us her blessing.

Marie-Pierre Colle

CHAPTER ONE

THE PRIMITIVE AND THE POPULAR

I n pre-Hispanic times the houses of peasants had but one room. Here, food was prepared (as it is in today's primitive houses) around a hearth built of three stones arranged to support a *comal* (earthenware pot). For sleeping, *petates* (reed mats) were rolled out. The room's other main use was the practice of religion. The early Mexicans were animistic, and they used a simple table as an altar for their offerings to a multitude of gods.

Materials used for houses varied according to availability. Walls might be made with brick, stone, adobe, or even living organ cactus in some desert areas. Roofs were made of tile, wood shingles, thatch, or the dried leaves of the agave. The Spanish introduced iron and the ax to Mexico, facilitating the construction of wood houses, such as those of Michoacán. These houses were known as *trojes* (granaries), because grain was stored in the roof. Earlier *trojes* were carved and embellished, and resembled similar housing in Russia and Scandinavia.

Most of these simple houses, built with the same materials and techniques, can still be found in Mexico today, as the country slowly enters the twentieth century.

O PPOSITE: This typical one-room *troje* (wooden house) in Michoacán has no windows. A table serves as family altar. Around the altar—with its statue of a saint, candles, and flowers—the wall is decorated with a display of pinups, mementos, and calendars, all illuminated by a single light bulb. The bedrooms and kitchen are in separate *trojes*.

RIGHT: Smoke from the fire in this typical Michoacán kitchen escapes through gaps in the roof. The walls have gaps for ventilation. Since pre-Hispanic times, there have been stoves like this made of three stones resting on the earthen floor. BELOW: The front verandah of this residential *troje* is for eating and socializing and is decorated with maize hanging to dry. *Trojes* stand in family compounds. Residential *trojes* are typically more elaborate than the kitchen or sleeping *trojes*.

TOP: A traditional *troje* kitchen, decorated with both utensils and ornamental pots. MIDDLE: The front verandah of this residential *troje* is unusually lavish in decoration. BOTTOM: A typical wall of adobe brick in Valle de Bravo.

L EFT, FROM TOP: The little colonial town of Tlacotalpan, famous for its vividly colored walls, was a favorite of Luis Barragán. A log cabin at Sebine, Michoacán. A tiled bench in the *zócalo* (main square) in Atlixco, Puebla, with a picture of village houses (perhaps in Oaxaca) that have thatched roofs. A simple thatched cottage in the fishing village of Mulegé in Baja California. BELOW: Another view of Tlacotalpan, Veracruz, where every house seems to be red, green, blue, yellow, pink, or purple. . . . OPPOSITE: A solitary musician plays below the wall of an old colonial house in the center of Pátzcuaro, Michoacán.

CHAPTER TWO

THE HACIENDA

T he haciendas were the landed estates of Mexico, some with territories as big as Belgium. For visitors to Mexico, they conjure up surreal images of ruined palaces, still possessing a faded grandeur, dominating a desolate landscape of cactus and agave. Before the revolution of 1910, when their lands were confiscated, the haciendas (a term which referred either to the estate or the often huge house of the owner) made up a high percentage of Mexico's agricultural land, and their collective power was enormous. Each one was a rural, autonomous social unit with its own history, and for each, myths accumulated over the centuries.

Haciendas were created under a system established in the sixteenth century, which bestowed land to conquistadores and other Spanish notables in exchange for military and social services to the crown. These land grants were limited to a few hundred acres, partly for security reasons (there was the fear, based on European experience, that huge estates might eventually pose a threat to national security). Over time these estates invariably grew. The *hacendado* (or owner) might buy neighboring ranches; often he would simply appropriate Indian land. As the haciendas grew they became feudal estates supplying all the needs of the surrounding community, including food, clothing, and medical aid.

Haciendas played host to a variety of activities from baptisms, weddings, and celebrations of saints' days to fiestas, *charro* (cowboy)

33

A niche in the adobe-walled stables at the hacienda of Chichimequillas, Querétaro, is a reminder of the constant presence of religion in Mexican life.

34

Decorative arches with indentations peculiar to the Querétaro region frame a balcony of the *casa grande* at the Chichimequillas hacienda.

parties and contests, bullfights, and harvest festivals. Travelers who stopped for the night, whether invited or not, were treated to displays of hospitality, particularly in the more remote regions, as described in this report from Santa Inés in 1828: "We arrived at about 3 o'clock . . . and the relics of the dinner brought forward for us. . . . We spent the afternoon in the shade on the terrace, chatting, smoking cigars with the ladies . . . the Marqués de Salvatierra, with his lady and family, the Marqués de Santiago, and his sister; miners, soldiers, lawyers—and priests, of course. Besides our worthy host, Don Antoñio de Michaus, we made the number of his guests twenty-four, and for the most part they had come—like ourselves—*au hasard*, uninvited and unexpected, but sure of a hearty welcome and good fare."

The *hacendado* and his wife had various responsibilities as community leaders. He might be called on to act as judge, and she often toured the estates, ministering to the sick with the simple remedies available at the time. Mescal was pressed into service as a

universal cure-all, from a rub down for sprains, to a treatment for colds and the grippe. Its virtues were summed up in a popular saying: "good for what ails you and also good if nothing ails you." It was even used as a measure of distance; the hard drinking *hacendados* often referred to a nearby village as "one bottle of mescal from home."

The *charro* played a similar role in the life and folklore of the hacienda as did the cowboy on the American ranch. His horsemanship skills, his elaborate and elegant clothing and accoutrements, his music, and his pride and personal style were every bit the equal of those of his cousins across the border. The tradition of the *charreada* (rodeo) is still kept alive in the haciendas of today, and the *charro* has become a symbol of nostalgia for the traditional rural life of Mexico.

For the Indian population whose lands had been appropriated by the hacendados, hacienda life was often less romantic and rosy than diaries describing social visits to the haciendas might suggest. De-

Top: The weathered, buttressed, early eighteenth-century walls of a hacienda's granary, with *ojo de buey* (oxeye) window opening. ABOVE: A figure of the infant Jesus in the Chichimequillas family chapel.

prived of their own land, the Indians were forced to work on the haciendas as peons, and had little choice but to buy everything they needed from the hacienda store, further increasing their dependency.

The relentless growth of the haciendas was not due to a need for, or even interest in, increased production but was usually motivated simply by the prestige that went with substantial land ownership. Only about 10 percent of hacienda land was ever cultivated. Once acquired, most of this land which had once been carefully cultivated by the Indians was left as derelict pasture.

Haciendas usually concentrated on one particular agricultural product, depending on the region: mescal in Zacatecas, sugar in Morelos, sisal in Yucatán, *pulque* (the alcoholic beverage produced from the agave plant which, when further distilled, becomes mescal) in Hidalgo, and cattle in Querétaro. Around the haciendas, and administered by them, were smaller ranches which supplied grain and other seasonal crops.

By the eighteenth century a typical hacienda was an elaborate institution. In addition to the main house and its guest quarters there were stables, a general store, a chapel, a school, equipment stores, servants' quarters, granaries, corrals, and a forge. Clothing was produced at the hacienda from cloth woven on the premises.

The haciendas grew in size during the centuries of colonial rule. In 1821 Mexico became an independent nation, but lapsed into a period of decline and economic upheaval. From 1864 to 1867 the French occupied Mexico with Maximilian and his wife Carlota installed as Emperor and Empress. This intervention was brief, but it began a period of French influence in architecture and culture which lasted well into the twentieth century.

From 1876 until 1911 Porfirio Díaz ruled Mexico as dictator, restoring it to economic strength by the use of capitalist measures and the encouragement of foreign investment.

Earlier in the nineteenth century there had been failed attempts by liberals to dissolve the haciendas and restore their land to the Indians. Díaz did the opposite, making extra land available to establish new haciendas and increasing the size of many existing ones. During his

OPPOSITE: A poinsettia flowering in a corner of a hacienda garden. TOP: Beside the entry gate of the hacienda of San Pedro Tejalpa is a peaceful canal, part of the hacienda's irrigation system. MIDDLE: A cactus garden. BOTTOM: The attractive eighteenth-century façade of the hacienda of Jajalpa.

rule many haciendas were given a face-lift, usually in the form of a proud neoclassical style reflecting the new national confidence.

Meanwhile, living conditions declined further for the majority of Indian peons working on the haciendas during the Díaz regime. It is a situation best described by Henry Bamford Parkes in his book *A History of Mexico*. "Courteous, sensual, and decadent, with charming manners and with nothing to live for except pleasure, the hacendados lived in the City of Mexico, or more often in Paris, drawing revenues from the lands which their ancestors had conquered or stolen from the Indians and leaving them to be managed by hired administrators. . . . When, once or twice a year, they visited their estates, the peons were given a holiday, and the owner and his wife would distribute gifts and pride themselves on the happy faces of their dependents. Of the actual lives of their peons, of how the administrators would beat them and torture them and claim feudal rights over their wives and daughters, these absentee owners remained blissfully unaware."

The revolution of 1910–1920 finished the haciendas. The enlisted troops of Pancho Villa, Venustiano Carranza, and Emiliano Zapata roamed the country, burning and pillaging every hacienda they could find. The lands were restored to the Indians and landowners subsequently were allowed only 200 acres.

Haciendas today are often still owned by descendants of the old *hacendados*. Others have been bought since the Revolution by Mexicans from the city wishing to have a place in the country, and some have become hotels and conference centers. Most of those which are occupied today have undergone complete renovation, since the burnings and sackings of the Revolution left some with little more than the basic walls.

TOP: The main façade and entry of the hacienda of Tenexac. MIDDLE: Brightly colored farm buildings of the hacienda of San Pedro Tejalpa. BOTTOM: A new use for discarded light bulbs—decorating the verandah of a caretaker's cottage in the hacienda of Jajalpa. OPPOSITE: In the distance, on axis with the agave-lined driveway, the Pyramid of the Sun at Teotihuacán looms majestically over the treetops at San Juan Tlacapecpan.

San Juan Tlacatecpan

A long straight driveway, flanked by fields of spiky agave, leads to the broad, neoclassical façade of San Juan Tlacatecpan (*Tlacatecpan* means "place of the Lord"). Built in the seventeenth century (the façade was added in 1857), San Juan Tlacatecpan's lands once comprised 16 million acres—an area bigger than the country of Belgium. The driveway is on axis with the Pyramid of the Sun at Teotihuacán, which is clearly visible in the distance over the treetops, and whose massive form lights up like a glowing coal on weekend nights as the ritual of *Son et Lumière* is enacted.

Beside the massive *portones* (entry doors) are terra cotta benches used by riders when dismounting; set into the wall are bronze horse heads with rings for tying up the horses.

The arched entrance leads through to a square patio lined on all sides by an arcade. In the center is a large decorative well, and there are cedar and agapanthus trees

O PPOSITE: Sheltered by the arcade surrounding the courtyard is a nineteenth-century carriage, a reminder of pre-Revolutionary days. ABOVE: A decorative painted stucco bench, surmounted by doves holding a wreath, is part of a pavilion next to the hacienda's swimming pool. LEFT: Used for tying up horses, this ring is built into the hacienda's main façade, next to the entrance.

offering additional shade. The *corredor* is arranged with shaded seating areas, and on one side there is a display of hats and saddles, each saddle fashioned of hand-tooled leather and silver and emblazoned with the name of the horse thy each belong to: Zacatecas, El Chopi, El Dorado, and El Zempasuchil.

The hacienda is decorated in an indigenous style. The doors, windows, and niches of the huge dining room are painted yellow; pots and plates from Puebla and ceramics from Guadalajara are displayed in the niches. At one end of the room there is a fruit bowl in relief, painted in the style of Frida Kahlo. The structural ceiling is a brick *boveda* (a vaulted technique traditional in the area in which bricks are laid with no underneath support). Next to the dining room is the picturesque kitchen, presided over by the resident cook and her family—a world within a world. There is a chapel inside the hacienda, and by its entrance is a niche with a virgin figure in a popular style, dressed in shocking pink.

The present owners, a prominent Mexico City businessman and his wife, have restored the hacienda with the aid of architect Alex von Wuthenau to a degree of comfort and nostalgia compatible with twentieth-century tastes.

PRECEDING PAGES: The agaves planted along the driveway bear witness to the hacienda's past: it produced the alcoholic beverage *pulque*. ABOVE: The *corredor* made it possible to spend one's day outside, sheltered from both sun and rain. The furniture is typical *rancho* style. Above it is an early enlarged photograph of the hacienda. The arcade was rebuilt with the help of architect Alex von Wuthenau. OPPOSITE: The magnificent dining room has a *boveda Catalana* made by artisans from Guanajuato to the pattern of the original, which was destroyed in the Revolution. The frescoes were painted by an Indian artist who copied patterns that date from the sixteenth century.

44

Opposite: The kitchen is illuminated by an *ojo de buey* (oxeye) window and decorated in the traditional manner with attractive pots, both large and miniature. The kitchen, despite its size, can cater a meal for three hundred people.

Two Indian girls, wearing their Sunday best, stand in front of a decorated carriage.

Hacienda Grande

Despite its name the Hacienda Grande is relatively modest in scale. It is located on the outskirts of Tequisquiapan, an attractively restored colonial spa town which is a popular destination for tourists from Mexico City.

The eighteenth-century façade of the hacienda faces both a large courtyard and the family chapel, which was added in 1850. The stone frame surrounding the entrance is decorated with a stylized undulating design representing Quetzalcoatl, the plumed serpent-god for whom Cortés was mistaken when he arrived in Mexico. On the door itself is a branding iron, the brand of which was established in 1694. There are the customary benches on each side of the doorway for riders to dismount. The interior courtyard is in the Andalusian style, with arches of gray Querétaro stone.

The cobbled exterior courtyard of the hacienda, with its eighteenth-century façade. The chapel to the left was added in 1850.

The hacienda was bought in 1908 by the grandfather of Carmen de la Mora, the present owner. At that time, just before the Revolution, the hacienda owned 70,000 acres of the surrounding countryside. This land had once been part of the territory of La Malinche, the guide and mistress of Hernán Cortés.

Hacienda Grande is a *ganadera* (bullfighting hacienda) and enjoys the reputation of supplying the best bulls in Mexico. Over the years at least 3,000 bulls from the hacienda have been sent to the Plaza de Toros in Mexico City.

The interiors of the hacienda were largely decorated in the nineteenth century and escaped destruction during the Revolution. They are filled with relics and faded photographs of bullfighting activities.

The dining room is Porfirian (late nineteenth century). It has stained glass windows, and the ceiling is finished in painted fabric with flowers around the edges fitted with tiny light bulbs. Originally there was also a chandelier, but this has been missing since the Revolution. Decorating the walls of the dining room are the heads of special champions, preserved in honor of

The *corredor* (covered porch) faces an attractive courtyard framed between stone columns.

their performance. On the right is Aceituno, who fought Manolo Martinez, one of Mexico's most illustrious bull-fighters, in what is known as the latter's greatest fight. Aceituno's head was also cast in bronze and can be seen over the entrance of the Plaza de Toros in Mexico City. The preserved head of Venadito, who was fought by Diego Puerta, now rests in peace above the buffet.

OPPOSITE: The late nineteenth-century Porfirian dining room lost its chandelier, but otherwise survived the Revolution. Hacienda Grande is famous for its fighting bulls, and heads preserved in honor of their performance in the *Plaza de Toros* in Mexico City are proudly displayed. Aceituno (seen on the right) is also cast in bronze over the main entrance of *Plaza de Toros*. ABOVE: The kitchen, with a traditional stove in the foreground and the traditional display of ornamental utensils.

Tenexac

Tenexac, a cattle hacienda and another leading supplier of fighting bulls, is an hour's drive from Puebla. Before the advent of the automobile it was a full day's ride to the nearest town and back with a horse and buggy. This trip was made once a week for supplies; a *tenate* (or large basket) was always taken to carry the bread, wrapped in avocado leaves to keep it fresh.

Tenexac is owned by Sabino Yano. An important conservationist and anthropologist in the state of Puebla, Yano is careful to see that his hacienda is maintained as close to its original condition as possible.

The hacienda was built in the nineteenth century, and when seen from a distance, set against a landscape of extinct volcanoes, it resembles a traditional *pueblo* (village). There is a main residence, a school, a church, houses for a teacher and for the Indian families, and a shop. The perimeter walls are made of volcanic rock and were built during a time of drought. The hacienda's readily available supply of *pulque* was used instead of water to make the mortar.

Unlike many other haciendas, Tenexac has been lived in by one family continuously. It was damaged less than most during the Revolution. To visit Tenexac is to step into the authentic past.

OPPOSITE: The calendar over this kitchen counter was left as a reminder of the year of Sabino Yano's parents' wedding. ABOVE: Lemonade is being prepared by a young Indian cook before the Sunday lunch. The kitchen is decorated with a frieze of *azulejos* from Puebla.

56

ABOVE: The nineteenth-century façade is reminiscent of a walled *pueblo*. The line of trees marks the main residence and the hacienda's entrance. LEFT: Here trees provide shade for an afternoon conference between the owner's mother and a farm manager. OPPOSITE: The nineteenth-century courtyard has a brick lattice balustrade, a central fountain, and a display of roses.

The interior of the hacienda has been kept by the family very much as it was at the turn of the century. The bedrooms extend along one side of the building. There is no internal corridor; instead the rooms open onto each other with a single bathroom at the end. To circumvent the problem of having to walk through all the bedrooms, including that of his mother, to get to the bathroom in the middle of the night, it would be simple and logical for Yano to build a corridor along the back. However, the building is listed as historic, so no such change is planned.

The bathroom—the only one in the house—is decorated with Austrian tiles, with floral decorations of marguerites and roses.

ABOVE: The tack room is filled with an assortment of riding gear. The display of cow skins show that this is a *ganadera* (cattle hacienda). LEFT: The dining room is ready for the Sunday lunch. Electricity reached Tenexac only in the early 1980s, and the earlier light fixtures still remain in place. OPPOSITE: The bedrooms are arranged enfilade, connected with each other by a line of doors. At the end of these is the solitary bathroom.

The kitchen is decorated with a frieze of Pueblan *azulejos* (tiles), and it features a stone water filter: the water falls through porous stones into a terra cotta pot. Sausages and smoked hams are made at the hacienda, and there is a mill for making tortillas.

OPPOSITE: The owner's bedroom is dominated by a brass bed. Decorated with a pineapple motif, it belonged to his great-grandparents, and many children have been born here over the generations. The crib is from Vienna and is filled with dolls which are family antiques. RIGHT: The bathroom is decorated with Austrian tiles. ABOVE: The drawing room seems untouched since the nineteenth century; its wallpaper, furniture, and chandelier are all original to the house.

La Laja

La Laja, near Querétaro, is unique among the early haciendas for the uncluttered lines of its almost minimalist architecture, particularly the entry courtyard and a remarkable colonnade facing the rear patio.

As with many haciendas, La Laja is a world unto itself, even today. A long drive through a landscape of maguey and cactus leads eventually through a portal into a magnificent courtyard, the walls of which are red and as linear as the work of Luis Barragán. La Laja was his favorite hacienda. The courtyard serves as a general reception area and meeting place; the chapel, main house, and stables are all entered from this courtyard. It can be peaceful one minute, and filled the next with the commotion of horses, their hooves crashing and sliding on the cobbles.

The hacienda's interior, which has been renovated by architect Juan Sordo Madaleno, is simple, with massive white walls and furniture in scale with the architecture. *Charro*-style striped rugs lie on layers of straw *petates*, the

traditional floor-covering in primitive homes. The dining room is dominated by an immense square table; when used for large dinner parties its surface is covered with a sea of candles.

The rear of the hacienda is distinguished architecturally by a sixteenth-century colonnade, behind which is a seating area furnished in a simple, traditional ranch style. The painted columns are without ornamentation, and they have collected an unforgettable patina. Enormous in diameter, their presence is such that the view of the patio they frame fades into insignificance. Behind the hacienda is a large swimming pool. Beyond the pool there is a large irrigated paddock full of calla lilies, providing enough to fill the house during their flowering season.

One of the resident horses enjoys a shampoo in the hacienda's venerable stables. OPPOSITE TOP: The stone-flagged main courtyard produces memorable echoes when the horses are brought in. As with much of Mexico's 16th century architecture, the lines are rectangular and pure: these are the lines that influenced Luis Barragan. BOTTOM: The 16th century entrance to the hacienda frames a long drive.

OPPOSITE: A covered
loggia facing the rear patio and garden has
an impressive sixteenth-century colonnade.
Some sense of the scale of the massive
vine-clad columns is given by the *equipal*
chairs.

The square dining
table seats sixteen and is set for dinner.
Behind the table is a large gold-leaf
painting by Mathias Goeritz. Everything in
this hacienda is kept very simple, but the
scale is massive and spectacular in effect.

San Pedro Tejalpa

San Pedro Tejalpa, near Toluca in the state of Mexico, was built in 1909, just before the Mexican Revolution, by Manuel Medina, a former Governor of the state of Mexico. Its function was to produce grain and cattle, although Medina also established a factory to weave wool in the hacienda. It was also Medina who introduced electric light to the city of Toluca—against the wishes of the city council. To overcome their opposition he placed the light posts on top of the roofs of houses instead of in the street.

Medina's son, Alfonso, sold the hacienda to its present owners. Alfonso is rumored to have locked himself inside the hacienda with his maid, who was also his lover. For twenty years he was seen by no one.

San Pedro Tejalpa is now owned by a French couple. Its neoclassical façade and courtyard show the French influence prevailing during the period of its conception. The interiors are attractively furnished in an appropriate *fin-de-siècle* style with many original features and fixtures.

Opposite: Built in 1909, just before the Revolution, San Pedro Tejalpa has a fine neoclassical façade, and is surrounded by pasture land. ABOVE: The courtyard shows the French influence prevalent at the time of the hacienda's design.

OPPOSITE: The view from the main bedroom through to the *sala* shows the *fin-de-siècle* decoration and ornate furniture of the period. ABOVE: Handsomely carved doorways link the living rooms. RIGHT: Contrasts in woman-hood—the matron, the madonna, and the huntress. The madonna dates from the eighteenth century and has a fine carved-ivory face.

ABOVE: The billiard room features a staircase leading to the tower above. The stair also provides bleacher space for spectators of the game. RIGHT: The dining room has an attractively patterned wood floor and typical *fin-de-siècle* furniture. The doorway leads to the kitchen, and the French doors on the right open onto the courtyard.

La Gavia

The original name of the hacienda La Gavia was Nuestra Senora de la Candelaria. Situated in an arid, rather cold region in the state of Mexico, its lands were originally granted by Hernán Cortés to his cousin, the Count of Santiago de Calimaya. In the eighteenth century ownership of the hacienda moved to the Jesuits who held it until they were expelled from Mexico in 1767. It was then bought at auction by the Count of Regla, the richest miner in Mexico.

In the nineteenth century, La Gavia came to prominence as a cattle and milk producer, known particularly for its milk, cream, and butter. It also possessed the most important collection of fighting cocks in the state of Mexico. But in the 1860s La Gavia temporarily lost its work force when they departed en masse to fight for Benito Juárez in his campaign against Maximilian. Doña Lola Riba y Cervantes owned the hacienda during the latter part of the nineteenth century and until she died in 1915. And, as with so many other haciendas, La Gavia was burned and ransacked during the Revolution.

A large wooden cross in the family chapel commemorates the death of Don Antonio Riba y Cervantes, son of Doña Lola, who inherited the hacienda during the Revolution. He was killed many years later when his plane hit a tree on the estate: his cross is made from branches broken off by the impact. The hacienda was then sold, in 1950, to José Ramón

TOP: The flamboyant entry gate is reached after navigating a small stream. ABOVE: The bullring wall is inset with steps designed for a quick exit. The distinctive rounded profile of old walls such as this has been used by contemporary architects such as José Yturbe. OPPOSITE: This door was rescued from a church altar which was about to be destroyed. It is surrounded by a painted fresco in the sixteenth-century manner, and with talavera tiles which were added by the father of the present owner.

Albarrán Pliego and his wife Estela, who were responsible for the restoration, furnishings, and present-day appearance of the hacienda.

An antiquarian and fanatical junk shopper, Albarrán amassed a huge collection of colonial paintings, antiques, and *objets d'art*, both good and bad. All of this is now distributed throughout the labyrinthine living rooms, salons, dining rooms, passages, and eighteen bedrooms of La Gavia. Albarrán covered the exterior with talavera tiles and other ornamentation where none had previously existed, changing its originally more restrained exterior to something more romantic and evocative.

La Gavia is on high ground and was once exposed to cold winds. Albarrán's other notable extravagance was a major tree-planting program which has surrounded the hacienda and the hill on which it stands with a forest, creating an even more private world than before. To add to the fantasy, he created a golf course and a lake.

Today, now that Albarrán is no longer alive, La Gavia is run by his son José. The hacienda is used for entertaining, often on a lavish scale, and as a family retreat.

Opposite: The exterior courtyard façade of La Gavia was embellished in the twentieth century, but it retains its eighteenth-century architectural character. Beyond the arches is the internal courtyard of the house. TOP: The *sala*, like much of the interior, has been furnished from junk-shop expeditions during the 1950s. The Chinese porcelain was part of shipments from China to Europe via Acapulco, much of which remained in Mexico. On the right is a copy of Velazquez's *La Fragua de Vulcano*. ABOVE: The flamboyant bedroom of José Ramón Albarrán Pliego, who was responsible for the restoration and interior decoration of La Gavia. Riding gear and pistols are hung on the bedposts.

Tenango

Founded at the beginning of the seventeenth century, Tenango, near Cuautla in the state of Morelos, was the first sugar hacienda in Mexico. The original owner, a Basque named Sabidigoitia, was a man of mean spirit but great charm. According to legend, he had made a pact with the devil and was able to appear in seven places at once. In order to do this, however, he had to keep seven cats locked up. One day, when he was off making simultaneous payments to the seven ranches that supplied him with the water necessary for the processing of his sugar, his wife let the cats out and Sabidigoitia was never seen again. However, in the eighteenth century the large figure portraying Sabidigoitia, making a characteristic gesture with his arms of a measure of payment, appeared on the roof of the hacienda, and it has remained there ever since.

In the nineteenth century the old sugar plant was replaced with a new one, and a new main house was built. Tenango's only rival as a sugar manufacturer was the ha-

The remains of the sugar factory. Its stone arches, now landscaped, have been made a part of the gardens at Tenango.

78

cienda of San Nicolás Tolentino in Puebla, owned by another branch of the same family. In 1889 both haciendas entered their products for the Paris International Exposition. The judges awarded first prize to Puebla and second prize to Tenango, apparently deciding that the Tenango sugar looked too white and therefore artificial. The fact that the *hacendado* from Puebla had also been the Mexican ambassador to France for 35 years might have also had an influence on the decision.

During the Revolution the hacienda was burned on three separate occasions by the troops of Zapata, whose headquarters were nearby: only the walls were left. The present owners are content with what has been a relatively basic restoration. Their accommodations (they live in Mexico City and visit on weekends) are neither luxurious nor grand, although they have built a large swimming pool next to the remains of the *bodega*.

ABOVE: Here one of the horses is being exercised in front of the nineteenth-century residential quarters. To the left is part of the old sugar factory. OPPOSITE: Part of the original seventeenth-century façade, which was damaged during the Revolution. Sabidigoitia, gesturing to indicate a measure of payment, is seen on the roof; the hacienda's chapel is in the background.

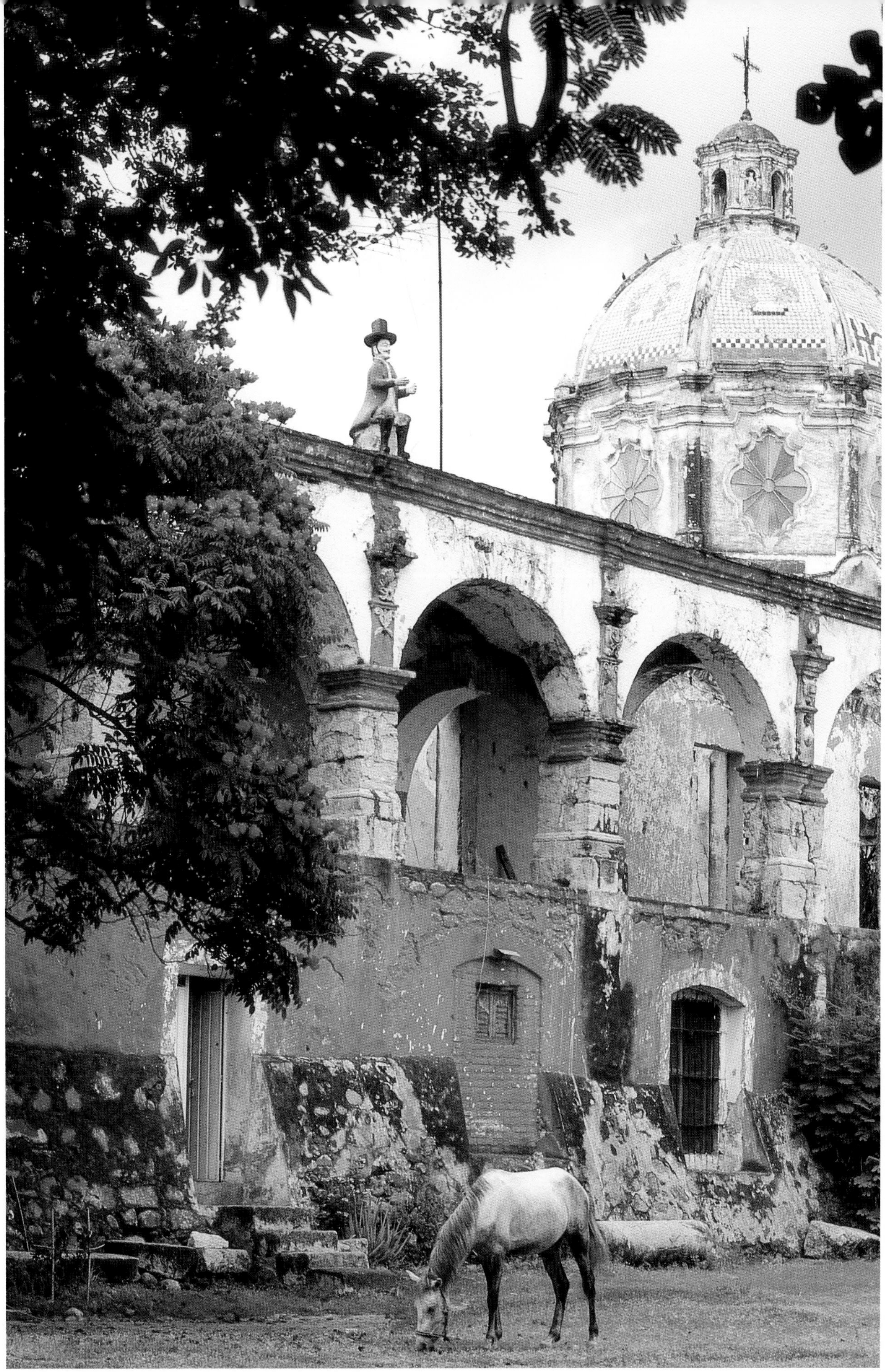

A New Hacienda

Designed by architect José de Yturbe for stockbroker Roberto Hernandez, this hacienda was built in the mid-1980s in the state of Mexico as a large family weekend retreat and also for the breeding of thoroughbred horses.

The stone-flagged courtyard—with its adobe walls and its large circular drinking trough—is a loving recreation of similar spaces in the traditional haciendas, with much of the simplicity and grandeur of La Laja (which was renovated by Yturbe's father-in-law, the architect Juan Sordo Madaleno).

The courtyard is entered through a low archway. The stone-floored space within serves as a distribution center for all the activities of the hacienda, and there is access from it directly to the house.

The stone floor is a guarantee that the usual acoustic characteristics of a hacienda courtyard will prevail: as soon as horses enter the space the clatter of hooves echoing from all four adobe walls is deafening but magical.

Opposite: An old wooden ladder gives some sense of the scale of the adobe walls and cobblestone floor of the interior courtyard. TOP: The hacienda's entrance, with the arched entrance to the interior courtyard, and the residence on the left. ABOVE: The main courtyard, looking toward the entry archway. In the center is a circular water trough for the horses. The massive low opening between the spaces is a deliberately modernist statement and draws attention to the traditional massive quality of the walls.

CHAPTER THREE

THE COLONIAL STYLE

I n 1519 Hernán Cortés and his fleet of adventurers arrived in Mexico, dropping anchor in what is now Veracruz. Within two years they had conquered the Aztec Empire and zealously set about colonizing the new territory in the name of Spain and converting its inhabitants to Christianity.

To achieve this, monks were summoned from Spain. Upon their arrival they dispersed across the countryside, assiduously building churches, monasteries, and cities. Such was the pace of this work (often a church would be built in a week) that by the end of the sixteenth century most of the Indian population had been baptized, nearly 500 new monasteries built, and a network of new cities, including such important centers as Puebla, Guadalajara, and Morelia, reached from one end of New Spain to the other.

There were few architects. The vast building program was instead supervised by monks who worked without blueprints, fashioning an improvised Hispanic architecture built of memories. The native Indian craftsmen and builders who were recruited to carry out the work were accustomed to monolithic Aztec masonry structures. European building techniques—which enclosed large spaces and did so with rela-

OPPOSITE: The Casa del Gigante. With an eye on the stairs and sword at the ready, this fierce soldier stands guard over the living quarters of this eighteenth-century mansion built on the main square of Pátzcuaro, in Michoacán.

Top: Massive simplicity is a keynote of early colonial architecture. ABOVE: The eighteenth-century Casa de los Azulejos (House of the Tiles) in Mexico City.

tively delicate arches, vaults, and column supports—amazed them. But they adapted quickly, as did the decorative craftsmen, who were forced to abandon their traditional motifs and learn new ones (although inevitable echoes of their own heritage resurfaced from time to time).

Housing as well as churches in colonial Mexico followed the Spanish model. Following Moorish tradition (Spain was long a part of the Moorish empire) the Spanish lived almost exclusively in towns, which provided security. The countryside in Mexico was divided up into the huge feudal estates known as haciendas, and the Indian population lived in separate *pueblos* (villages). The typical colonial house was a town house, and in many ways it was not so different from the houses of pre-Hispanic Mexico. These houses were inward-looking, presenting blank faces, and around them were walled gardens. Rooms were assembled around internal courtyards, which often had colonnades. The houses had fireplaces with stone chimneys.

The colonial house may have been influenced by these pre-Hispanic models, but its main antecedents could be traced back via the Moors to Carthage and Rome. Usually of two stories (to save space) and arranged around a courtyard, the colonial house was located in a street.

The street itself was a simple corridor. Each house presented an inscrutable walled façade with windows masked by decorative iron grillwork reflecting the Moorish desire to protect the family from the outside world. A large portal with a pair of massive doors sufficiently wide to admit a carriage provided access to the private world within.

In contrast to this impersonal exterior, the inner courtyard was, and still is, a vivid microcosm of Mexican life. It gave both light and focus to domestic activities. It was usually animated by water splashing from a central fountain of Mudéjar design (Mudéjar is the name given to the style developed by Moors who remained in Spain after the Christian reconquest).

The baroque façade of a house in Apaseo el Grande, a small village near Querétaro. Houses of this style are rare in Mexico.

A stone stairway, which was formal and monumental in more important houses, led to the living quarters on the upper floor, where there were drawing rooms and sitting rooms, the dining room, and bedrooms. At the rear and below was the kitchen and bathroom, servants' quarters and stables.

This then was the basic colonial house. The more lavish houses occupied the central square and its immediate surroundings; houses in the outskirts were simpler. Often there were decorative variations from town to town. Puebla for example was the center of a growing tile industry. There buildings were dressed inside and out with a profusion of brightly colored tiles (*azulejos*). Elsewhere, distinctions were more subtle. But the buildings of particular towns could be distinguished by architectural details and varieties of stone.

During this colonial period, which spanned three centuries (1521–1821), many important developments were made in architecture in Europe. These changes were slow in reaching Mexico, and until the eighteenth century only the most marginal evolutionary developments were reflected in the Mexican house.

The eighteenth century was a period of great prosperity in Mexico. Two preceding centuries of peace and progress in agriculture, mining, and industrial activities had made Mexico the envy of European nations which were torn by wars. Mexico City with its wide boulevards came to be known during this period as the City of Palaces, as more and more grand houses were built and refurbished with a lavishness of ornamentation reflecting familial pride and success.

Making all this possible was a feudal system that relied on the availability of cheap Indian labor. This was, of course, not to last forever. But during this colonial era there was no hint of the revolution that would take place a full century after the end of Spanish rule.

The baroque reached Mexico in the early eighteenth century and was embraced by Mexican designers with more enthusiasm than had been the case with earlier styles. A Spanish variant known as Churrigueresque, named after a Spanish family of architects, became very popular. It was taken so much further than its Spanish antecedent that it became the first and the boldest manifestation of a purely Mexican

Opposite: The extraordinary living room of the Casa Bello in Puebla. The walls are decorated with tiles and bricks interspersed with *rosetones* (stucco flowers). Large *azulejos* panels show San Miguel and San Francisco. TOP: A seventeenth-century fountain in the garden of Fernando and Rosalba Ortiz Monasterio's house in Coyoacán. ABOVE: A vine-clad tower in the garden of a house in San Miguel de Allende.

architecture. Displaying a lavishness of decorative detail rather than the manipulation of form and space, indigenous craftsmen were finally expressing themselves in a way that was exotic and convincingly non-European.

While Mexican baroque is more often associated with a spectacular series of churches in the older colonial cities, the style was occasionally translated into houses. The façade of the Casa de los Perros ("House of the Dogs") in the town of Apaseo el Grande near Querétaro is one of the best remaining examples of the baroque in residential architecture.

The colonial period ended with the signing of the *Plan de Iguala* in 1821. During the nineteenth century Mexico was opened to foreigners for the first time and architecture began to reflect newly introduced neoclassical influences, first from Italy and then from France. The former was largely limited to the inappropriate neoclassical renovation of a number of baroque churches by groups of Italian architects. The French style, which first appeared during the reign of Maximilian and reached its zenith during the Porfirian years was more deep-rooted. During this period newly-built houses, palaces, haciendas, and residential interiors all looked as if they had strayed from the French provinces.

The Mexican colonial house did not die, however, and examples of the style continued to be built into the twentieth century. Some of its spirit has been revived more recently by several architects who work in an eclectic traditional idiom nonetheless referred to as the colonial style. Foremost among these are Manuel Parra and Alex von Wuthenau (who arrived in Mexico from his native Germany in the 1930s).

T OP: Part of the façade of a church in Guanajuato. MIDDLE: Stone paving in the driveway of a house in Guanajuato. BOTTOM: A fine eighteenth-century façade in San Miguel de Allende.

LEFT: The *corredor* (covered porch) of Marie-Pierre Colle's house in Tepoztlán forms the nucleus of family life; it allows one to be outside but sheltered from the rain. The architect is Alex von Wuthenau. BELOW AND BELOW LEFT: The living room of Patricia Bubela's house in San Miguel, with a fine fluted fireplace, Mexican colonial furniture, and an eighteenth-century polychromed wood Madonna.

The Colonial Spirit

The houses of Manuel Parra invariably carry his personal signature. Such early examples as this house built in 1956 for the Riley family were designed using material salvaged from the myriad ruined convents and monasteries that dot the Mexican landscape. For a time this was available free to anyone who wished to take it. (Salvaged wood and stone are now an expensive commodity.) The interior and exterior walls, fireplaces, and balustrades were assembled in a collagelike arrangement of antique stone and brick, and the exposed interior beams were of recycled timber. In this way it was possible to produce a lavishly equipped house quite inexpensively—one that was new, but at the same time old in spirit and literally imbued with the colonial history of Mexico.

Having established a strong sense of the colonial period with his use of materials, Parra steers a more personal direction in his articulation of space and in the proportion of his rooms. In the Riley house the interior volumes are linked together by a rhythm of con-

Top: The entrance lobby is equipped with a washbasin taken from a provincial hotel. Above it is a gilded sunburst and next to it, a small colonial portrait. ABOVE: The space between the sitting and dining areas is linked by brick arches. The armchairs were made in Taxco, and the floor is lined with traditional *petates*. OPPOSITE: The upstairs landing links the bedrooms. The ceiling is painted with a traditional pattern. A pre-Columbian piece rests in a small niche.

nected arches, while stone stairs spill and curve in a gentle, almost free-form manner.

The Riley house is in San Angel and its owner, Beach Riley, is a retired American engineer and fabric manufacturer who has spent most of his working career in Mexico. He has been closely connected with many of its leading architects, particularly Luis Barragán, providing the fabric for some of his interiors. The house is on a picturesque cobbled street characteristic of San Angel, with high walls behind which the foliage of huge trees suggests hidden gardens of generous proportions. The street door is set in a wall of rustic brick. Inside this wall is a tiny patio; stone steps lead up to the house, which is partially hidden by a miniature jungle of vines and potted plants. The effect is mysterious rather than picturesque.

The lobby within is the circulation hub for the house. From here there is a diagonal view, articulated by a progression of arches into the sitting room. To the left a stairway leads upstairs to the bedrooms, and to the right there is a study. The dining room, sitting room, and study are all linked by the system of arches and anchored by an attractive and unusual fireplace. The living and dining rooms open onto a small, shady garden.

OPPOSITE: An attractive Virgin of Guadalupe rests in a colonial frame and is supported by a stone from a demolished building. Most of the beams, stonework, and flooring came from demolition sites. ABOVE LEFT: Lines in the stucco decorate the fireplace chimney. On the mantelpiece are pre-Columbian figures from Veracruz and Nayarit. The painting is by Pedro Alvarado. ABOVE: The entry steps with stonework recycled from old demolished colonial buildings.

Rekindling the Past

Once part of a *rancho* producing maguey (*pulque*, an alcoholic drink, is made from this spiky agave) the Saldivars' eighteenth-century house is no longer surrounded by countryside. Today it is in the middle of the busy, part-commercial and part-residential district of Tizapán in the southern part of Mexico City. The house was in ruins when Antonio and Francesca Saldivar bought it, and it has been carefully restored by architect Alex von Wuthenau to be close in spirit to the original.

The eighteenth-century entrance of volcanic stone opens into a cobbled front patio dominated by a seventeenth-century watchtower and shaded by a large jacaranda tree. Inside the front door is a large hallway whose windows overlook the back garden, with its colonial fountain and rustic walls.

The living room is at the east end of the hall, while at the other end there are bedrooms and family rooms reached by an attractive stone staircase. The living room is distinguished by a pair of re-

O<small>PPOSITE</small>: This eighteenth-century window is surmounted by an excellent *concha*—the popular shell shape said to bring blessings to the house. The painted decorations are original and have been restored. LEFT: A colonial fountain is the focal point of the back patio; behind the patio is a walled garden. BELOW: A large passageway/sitting area has a view of the garden and leads through to the main living room to the right and the dining room to the left.

cessed windows surmounted by *conchas* (stuccoed shell shapes which are said to bring blessings to the house, and which are a familiar motif in colonial interiors). The painted decorations around the windows are original and have been restored. Between these windows is a niche occupied by a seventeenth-century wooden figure of St. Santiago, who drove the Moors out of Spain in the fifteenth century.

A tunnel-like opening leads from the living room through the thick walls of the watchtower into its interior which is now a 25-foot-high dining room. High above a Wuthenau-designed dining table and seventeenth-century chairs is a minstrels' gallery where a string quartet often plays during dinner parties. (Francesca Saldivar is the organizer of an annual international music festival.)

OPPOSITE: The dining room is set inside the massive walls of a seventeenth-century watchtower. Above is a minstrels' gallery from which dinner guests are often serenaded by a string quartet. RIGHT: Seventeenth-century chairs surround a dining table designed by Alex von Wuthenau. ABOVE: An attractive colonial staircase leads to bedrooms.

Architect's Oasis

Alex von Wuthenau built his studio near San Angel next to a busy highway intersection. Its heavy stone façade looks two hundred years old, but is less than twenty-five. It acts as the necessary acoustic break: once ensconced within the baronial doors one immediately loses any sense of twentieth-century urban chaos.

In addition to his architectural activities, von Wuthenau is an ecologist and archaeologist of note. In fact his studio is a repository for over 80 years of intense activity in many directions. One senses that it was given so generous a scale to accommodate the overlapping of his many simultaneous interests, and in particular, a large collection of pre-Columbian heads and figures.

Aʙᴏᴠᴇ: Architect Alex von Wuthenau built his San Angel studio in the colonial style. The staircase is similar to those of old monasteries. Von Wuthenau is also an ecologist and anthropologist, and lives surrounded by his collections. ʟᴇғᴛ: The exterior faces a quiet garden. ᴏᴘᴘᴏsɪᴛᴇ: The mantel, surmounted by a colonial painting, has become a repository for Wuthenau's artifacts and mementos, displayed in Bloomsbury-like disorder.

The Moorish Influence

San Miguel de Allende, which is four hours drive north of Mexico City, has long attracted writers and artists who have settled in many of its prettier colonial houses. Its charms are such that it was made a national monument. It has been quietly and carefully restored, and protected from anything out of character. Its streets are almost universally cobbled, and yet avoid being overly picturesque.

The American fashion photographer Deborah Turbeville fell in love with San Miguel and found a house for herself which is being restored with the assistance of San Miguel-based designer Patricia Bubela. It is a simple one-story colonial house on a rough cobbled street, with a façade covered by a blue wash. What had made the house irresistible was its courtyard, with an unusual Moorish colonnade and a fresco featuring scenes from the Bible. The main living rooms open onto this space, which is animated by an attractive pond and fountain.

Above: Deborah Turbeville's Moorish courtyard, looking toward the entry archway. The walls are covered with a fresco of Biblical scenes. LEFT: The façade is typical of San Miguel, but has a distinctive blue wash. OPPOSITE: The courtyard's colonnade is framed by a passage leading back to the studio and guestrooms. Above is a large roof terrace.

LEFT: The Moorish courtyard with its frescoes of scenes from the Bible. BELOW: Dove cages rest on a colonial chest in a corner of the courtyard. OPPOSITE: The roof terrace of the Casa del Obelisco, with its view of the pseudo-Gothic cathedral. In the midst of a landscape of potted plants can be seen a small cupola, faced with talavera tiles, which acts as a skylight for the living room below.

Patricia Bubela has completed the design, restoration, and other extensive reconstruction of over 30 houses in San Miguel. One of these is the Casa del Obelisco, renovated for a family from France. Its most striking feature is its roof terrace. Colonial houses usually have flat roofs which are put to use in one way or another. In this case, the terrace is used as a place to view the cathedral, San Miguel's most celebrated if eccentric landmark. The inspiration for its nineteenth-century design was a postcard of a European cathedral.

B ELOW, FROM TOP:
The graceful proportions of an eighteenth-
century palace courtyard. A typical rural
landscape near the city of Querétaro. The
fountain in an ex-convent patio, Querétaro.
RIGHT: The eighteenth-century ex-convent of
San Augustin, Querétaro.

Querétaro

Querétaro, both a city and a state, is to the north of Mexico City. A trip to the city by car takes three hours; by train the trip is a bit longer, but it is pleasant to take advantage of the newly inaugurated early morning train (bright blue and all Pullman). An excellent breakfast is served as the train skims gently past cactus and arroyo before arriving in Querétaro on its way to San Miguel de Allende, its final destination.

The state of Querétaro lies in the center of Mexico and shares a plateau known as the Bajio with its neighbor, Guanajuato. Here, maize, vegetables, and fruit are produced. Querétaro is also a bullfighting center.

Querétaro is an attractive city, known for its colonial architecture with distinctive honey-colored stonework. Cars are banned from the old colonial center, which has been cleaned and restored. Attractive squares, linked by pedestrian streets, are edged by handsome palaces and houses. And the convents and churches of Querétaro are among the best in the country.

Cᴌᴏᴄᴋᴡɪsᴇ, ꜰʀᴏᴍ ᴛᴏᴘ ʟᴇꜰᴛ: An elaborately carved eighteenth-century fountain in the palace courtyard. A ceiling detail from the upper-level *corredor* in the courtyard of the eighteenth-century palace. Decorated stucco molding in the palace courtyard. A street corner in the center of town. The ornately carved courtyard of La Casa de la Marquesa. ʀɪɢʜᴛ: A venerable door in Querétaro with a cluster of bronze bossed nail heads and bronze knocker.

Casa de la Torre

From the time of Cortés, people were attracted to Cuernavaca because its climate is perfect year-round. The Casa de la Torre nestles below the walls of the sixteenth-century cathedral of Cuernavaca and was originally part of the Bishop's palace. Renovated by artist Robert Brady, it is dominated by the massive tower which gave the house its name.

Entering from the street, one climbs steep steps to the exotic patio, which achieves a harmony of scale despite the potentially daunting verticality of the cathedral. Varieties of cacti and tropical foliage have grown to giant proportions, thanks to the temperate climate. The patio is overlooked by the balcony of Brady's design studio, which is built into the cathedral wall. Facing the balcony is a formal flight of steps leading up to the main sala within the tower. Below these steps is a grotto-like fountain set into the wall beneath the balustrade and surrounded by orchids and moss.

Opposite: The recessed range in the Brady kitchen is framed by black and yellow *talavera* tile from Puebla, and protected from evil spirits by strings of garlic. Above the range is the tiled image of St. Pasenal, the patron saint of the kitchen. ABOVE: The tower was once a part of the Bishop of Cuernevaca's palace in the sixteenth-century cathedral compound. A large *huamuchil* tree shades the staircase. LEFT: The pool is decorated with *talavera*.

Frozen in Time

Across the street from the Casa de la Torre is the Cortina residence. The street itself is a narrow, bustling, downtown street, and consequently the first glimpse of the Cortina garden, which is visible the moment that the street door is opened, is startling. The house is U-shaped, and wraps around the top end of a substantial lawn, which slopes gently down to a distant pool and group of trees. Beyond this, the downward slope continues and both the house and the garden enjoy views extending to a fertile valley and distant hills, and the even more distant snow-capped twin peaks of Popocatepétl and Iztaccíhuatl (the smoky mountain and the sleeping woman), two giant volcanoes that dominate the central valley.

The house is seventeenth-century, with more recent additions, including those by interior designer Eduardo Bolio y Rendon. The owners, Joaquin Cortina Goribar and his wife Tana, are from old, established local families, and the house reflects their family history.

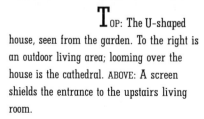

Top: The U-shaped house, seen from the garden. To the right is an outdoor living area; looming over the house is the cathedral. ABOVE: A screen shields the entrance to the upstairs living room.

ABOVE: A corner of the dining room. OPPOSITE: The entry steps, leading up from the street door.

LEFT: The dining room, with its Baccarat chandelier and the family's distinctive yellow china from Puebla. BELOW LEFT: A nineteenth-century portrait of the family posing in front of the cathedral in Mexico City. OPPOSITE: The kitchen, with its simple but striking use of tiles.

The Cortinas divide their time between Cuernavaca and their other house in Mexico City. Much of their life in Cuernavaca is spent in the garden room, a semi-enclosed patio area facing the garden. This is arranged informally with a display of china mounted on the back wall, but with no hint of the decorating flourishes which occur within the house itself.

A broad *corredor* (covered porch) provides shelter during the summer rains. The dining room is divided from this only by a heavy, brocaded curtain. (Doors and windows are not strictly necessary in this kindest of climates.)

The house is decorated in such a way that the past and present are seemingly intertwined. Heirlooms of previous generations mingle with those of the present owners' already long life together. In the dining room, the strange, sweet col-

ors are distinctively Mexican, both in their intensity and in the magic of their unexpected combinations. Over the dresser are marble busts of the present owners, by the same Cuernavaca sculptor, but unexpectedly done before the couple had been introduced to each other.

Cobalt blue stairs lead from the dining room to the upper living floor where the large, airy living room is situated—the better to enjoy the view of the volcanoes. There is a French influence in the curved lines of the decoration. The room and its decor has an ethereal quality and leaves one with a sense of being frozen in time—not inappropriate in Mexico, where the past and the present coexist harmoniously.

OPPOSITE: Another view of the kitchen. The fresco romantically links the names of the owners. Beyond is a small exterior courtyard. RIGHT, FROM TOP: Thanks to the temperate climate, the large window opening in the upstairs sitting room is unglazed. Decorative nineteenth-century glass is displayed on a painted cabinet. A detail of one end of the sitting room.

OVERLEAF: The sitting room is separated by a large arch, and each side is treated with a different decorative theme, one blue and the other pink. This end is dominated by a collection of framed fans.

118

CHAPTER FOUR

THE FRENCH INFLUENCE

H aving achieved its independence from Spain in 1821, Mexico slid into a period of economic decline, highlighted by anarchy, civil war, and a confrontation with the United States resulting in Mexico's loss of Texas and California. Spain, England, and France became involved in Mexico's internal problems, because of the latter's various unpaid debts and also because of their own foreign policy ambitions.

In 1864, after deciding that Mexico needed to be rescued from its problems, Napoleon III installed an army and appointed Maximilian, younger brother of the Habsburg Emperor of Austria, as a puppet emperor of Mexico.

Ensconcing themselves in the old colonial castle of Chapultepec on the western edge of Mexico City, Maximilian and his wife Carlota set about establishing a European-style court. The castle itself was transformed at great expense into a veritable palace, while a similarly lavish budget was spent on commissioning royal portraits and a succession of banquets and balls.

Unfortunately Maximilian had no experience of, and even less instinct for, politics, and failed to balance the various factions which

OPPOSITE: An art-nouveau balcony in Guanajuato.

120

Cut-stone balconies with delicate iron detailing on a late nineteenth-century neoclassical façade in Guanajuato.

had precipitated the country's continued unrest, or to find ways to replenish the bankrupt treasury—which was all the poorer due to a mandate to pay France back within two years for the costs of its Mexican invasion.

In 1865 Napoleon, realizing that Maximilian was ineffective, and under pressure from the United States to give up Mexico, abandoned his financial support and began to withdraw his troops. Maximilian stayed firm in his desire to stay in his adopted country despite the temptation to do the prudent thing—which was to leave. Carlota traveled to Europe to plead for support for her husband. She failed in this and eventually lost her mind, finishing her life in Belgium, referring to her husband as the "sovereign of the universe." Maximilian was captured by the troops of Benito Juárez, court-martialed, and executed. He was thirty-five, and he had been in Mexico for exactly three years.

Despite the brevity of his reign in Mexico, Maximilian helped create an appetite for French culture which was to remain until well into the twentieth century.

Porfirio Díaz ruled Mexico from 1876 to 1911. A strong, effective leader, he restored the country to peace and economic strength. Encouraging European and American investment, he developed industry and transportation, steering Mexico into the twentieth century. The influx of European money into Mexico brought with it a continuing appetite for all things European, and particularly French. The fashionable boulevards of Mexico City, especially the new Paseo de la Reforma (planned by Maximilian) became lined with magnificent French mansions and palaces in the neoclassical style.

Houses were invariably decorated in the French style, and the walls hung with the work of Parisian salon painters. The more sophisticated art-nouveau style, popular in Europe, made its appearance infrequently in Mexico, where the neoclassical style remained in favor.

Díaz was finally ousted in 1911, by which time the Revolution had begun. The first post-Revolutionary government, led by Alvaro Obregón, sought to establish a sense of national identity for the new Republic. He did so by encouraging Mexico to examine its own cultural roots; in 1921 he opened an exhibition of Indian crafts. His education minister, José Vasconcelos, established the famous Muralist program which sought to show Mexicans that their heritage was indigenous, not imported from Paris. Enlisting the contributions of the leading Mexican artists, including Diego Rivera, David Alfaro Siquieros, and José Clemente Orozco, Vasconcelos started an intellectual movement which galvanized the arts of Mexico and resurrected its indigenous culture. Artists such as Rivera, Rufino Tamayo, and Chucho Reyes began collections of pre-Hispanic art and decorated their homes in the "popular" Indian style. Because of their influence, interior decorators began to use Mexican colonial and indigenous furniture and art instead of shopping in Paris.

TOP: An imposing Porfirian town house in Mexico City. ABOVE: The façade of an elegant art-nouveau house in Guanajuato.

Poblano Neoclassical

The Casa Bello, now a museum, is a late nineteenth-century house in the Porfirian style in the center of Puebla, near the *zócalo*.

More colonial in style, the dining room is stylistically different from the rest of the house (see page 86), and pays spectacular homage to Puebla's tile-making industry. But apart from that one room, the house—with its delicate, moody colors, neoclassical detailing, and glazed courtyard canopies—seems transplanted from some unidentified town in provincial France. A large, rather institutional staircase, illuminated by an abundance of stained glass, leads up to the second level. Here, a balcony with a wrought-iron balustrade, sheltered by a glass canopy, overlooks a courtyard too small to conform to the usual Spanish colonial pattern. Presiding over this space is a bust of Napoleon III, placed in a formal niche. Opening onto the balcony are various living rooms and bedrooms.

Above: The second-floor balcony of the Casa Bello in Puebla, now a museum. The decoration and the glazed canopy are distinctively French. LEFT: The bust is of Napoleon I. OPPOSITE: The stairway shows typical nineteenth-century detailing. An Italian marble sculpture provides a focal point.

Fin-de-Siècle Morelia

José Alfonso Mier y Cortés lives in the house built in the late nineteenth century by his ancestors; he has lovingly restored it to its original *fin-de-siécle* condition. Located in the center of Morelia, it was built during the period when the city was enjoying a new prosperity derived from its mining industry. The style of the house represents the prevailing French influence in the arts which found a particularly strong expression in Morelia. Much of the furniture, paintings, and art objects in the house have been added by Cortés, who is an antiquarian.

The single-story house is laid out in the traditional manner established in the earlier colonial period, and the courtyard is decorated with potted plants and a large stone fountain. In the warm climate of Morelia, an internal corridor is unnecessary, and the courtyard itself is used for general circulation from one part of the house to another. Cortés is an expert pianist and the sounds of Chopin emanating from his grand piano make a perfect counterpoint to the architecture.

OPPOSITE: The ornate *corredor*, colonial in proportion but *fin-de-siècle* in its detailing. The rocking chair faces a patio with a fountain. ABOVE: A passerby complements the architectural features of the house, which is in the old colonial center of Morelia, a city that was much developed in the nineteenth century. The patio can be glimpsed through the open doorway.

OPPOSITE: The living
room, beautifully restored by its present
owner. An antiquarian, he has added to the
family's original furniture and *objets d'art*.
ABOVE: The owner's bedroom. Everything
has been restored to its original condition at
the end of the last century.

Jardin de la Rozière

Mexicans are not known for their ornamental gardens. The Spanish left behind a remarkable legacy of architecture and patios, but failed to leave any perceptible gardening heritage. Yet even if not so today, the Mexicans were once a race of gardeners. Warwick Bray, in his book *Everyday Life of the Aztecs* writes: "The palace of Nezahualcóyotl was surrounded by pine trees, interspersed with pavilions, mazes, lakes, and bathing places. Still more beautiful were the gardens of Nezahualcóyotl's retreat at Tetzcotzinco. An aqueduct carried water from the mountains into a reservoir ornamented with bas-reliefs, and from there it flowed by streams and canals all over the garden, filling the lakes and the bathing pools cut into the living rock. The remains of these basins can still be seen today, but no trace is left of the waterfalls, trees, birdcages, and flowerbeds which gave the king such delight. Montezuma had a similar garden at Huaxtepec which he filled with tropical flowers and young trees sent from the coast."

Sonia de la Rozière's pretty garden in Mexico City is as French as her *fin-de-siècle* house which it complements perfectly. The focal point of the garden is a shell-shaped pool and fountain backed by a high wall of volcanic rock planted with orchids. The pool is framed by two mature jacarandas which leave a carpet of blue flowers during the months of March and April. Between a paved patio and the pool is an arrangement of formal box hedges.

Aʙᴏᴠᴇ: A young jacaranda and a sculpted hedge. ʀɪɢʜᴛ: The shell-shaped pool is framed by a pair of old jacarandas which cover the formal box hedges with blossoms. To the left is a shell-shaped fountain, and inset into the high wall of volcanic rock are a multitude of orchids.

Palais Palma

The Palma family lives in an elegant *petit palais* situated on a busy street in the Colonia Roma, built in 1920 by architect Gustavo Peñasco. During this period the fashionable streets of Mexico City were lined with French-style mansions, and this is a fine surviving example.

Bought by Alejandro and Rosa Palma after the 1985 earthquake, the house has been renovated by the latter, who has for some time designed the interiors for architect Ricardo Legorreta's hotel projects. The house has been meticulously furnished in a style appropriate to the period of its original construction, with Mexican Chippendale furniture (popular during the late eighteenth century) and decorative objects from France.

Most of the paintings are by Angel Zarraga, a Mexican artist who was a contemporary of Diego Rivera, and a relative of the Palma family. Ostracized by the powerful left-wing Rivera clique for his failure to exhibit the requisite

OPPOSITE: Flanked by two Mexican chairs in the Chippendale style is a table, also Mexican, supporting a collection of French art-nouveau glass. ABOVE: The sitting room, with a 1915 painting by Mexican artist Angel Zarraga. LEFT: Another painting—this of soccer players and also in the sitting room—by Zarraga.

radical affiliations (he had too many right-wing friends), his work has only recently been favorably reappraised.

LEFT: The elegant bathroom, decorated in the fin-de-siècle style. BELOW: A sideboard with French silver and a Zarraga painting. OPPOSITE: The bedroom with a large colonial painting; the hammock is from Mérida.

The neoclassical and typically Porfirian house is on a busy street in what was once a predominantly French neighborhood in the middle of Mexico City.

1930s Splendide

This house was built in 1920 by the architect Marquina and has a neoclassical façade reflecting the importance of its original owner, who was a member of the family of Porfirio Díaz. It is separated from the street by a small garden; it has three floors, the third used as a small screening theater. Stained-glass windows which face the street were made for the house in Austria.

The interiors of the house were designed and supervised by Rosa Palma. Floors were replaced, and the whole building extensively renovated.

The conservatory was opened to the dining room to provide a continuous vista through the house, which is terminated in high-style by the magnificent, newly restored art-deco fountain, originally designed and added to the house in 1930 by Marquina.

136

ABOVE: A spectacular vista from the sitting room. Beyond the dining room, and framed by marble neoclassical columns, is the pretty art-deco fountain. OPPOSITE: A detail of the fountain. The sconce is fashioned of stained glass.

OVERLEAF LEFT: Adjacent to the fountain, a glazed screen opens onto a small terrace. RIGHT: Palma's bathroom, with one of the many stained-glass windows that face the street.

CHAPTER FIVE

THE HOMES OF ARTISTS

141

O ne of the earliest and most significant consequences of the Mexican Revolution of 1910–1920 was the birth of a new spirit of nationalism, and the beginnings of a quest for cultural identity. This quest became an important agenda for the post-Revolutionary government. One of its more remarkable features was the prominent role played in these matters by the country's leading artists.

In an attempt to resurrect the native Mexican culture—both pre-Hispanic and contemporary, with its rich traditions of arts, decorative crafts, music, and festivals—a series of major educational programs, including the painting of murals on public buildings, was adopted in 1920 by José Vasconcelos, the post-Revolutionary minister of education. These were created to teach the people of Mexico more about their roots and traditions, and to revitalize the productivity of native artists and craftsmen.

One of the artists who was attracted to the Muralist program (as it became known) was Diego Rivera. Rivera had just spent eleven years in Paris, studying Italian Renaissance frescoes, and he became aware that the mural could play an important role educationally. He saw it as a "visual book" and as "art for the masses," a concept particularly

OPPOSITE: The colors of Mexico are well represented in this corner of Frida Kahlo's dining room. Set in a niche of *azul añil* (a traditional matte wall paint) is a hand-painted fruit bowl with painted, lacquered wooden fruit which have been glued onto the wall. Below this, two carved wooden figures by the folk artist Mardonio Magaña rest against the wall; next to this are lacquered *guajes* from Michoacán. The tin church ornaments are from San Miguel de Allende.

This table-top assemblage of stuffed birds, pre-Columbian jade earrings, and a ceramic monkey is next to a living-room window facing the garden of the Olga and Rufino Tamayo house in San Angel.

attractive at a time when intellectuals identified strongly with the struggles of the proletariat both in Mexico and the Soviet Union. Upon his return to Mexico in 1921 he was struck by the "inexpressible beauty of this rich and severe, wretched and exuberant land," and early in 1922 he began work on *Creation*. This was the first of the murals that, together with those produced by José Clemente Orozco, David Alfaro Siqueiros, and others, were to give international recognition to the Muralist program. Inspired by this spirit of nationalism, most Mexican artists began to paint Mexican themes, rejecting European avant garde art as "elitist."

The themes that preoccupied the Muralists during the 1920s— depicting the history and struggles of the Mexican Indian—were to remain dominant in Rivera's work throughout his career. He became a

major collector of pre-Hispanic idol figures and jewelry, and the house he shared with Frida Kahlo in Coyoacán was decorated religiously with "popular" crafts and handicrafts bought in the village markets around the country.

Thanks partly to the influence of this early group of politically motivated artists and intellectuals, and also particularly to Jesús "Chucho" Reyes, another artist who was less political but no less a spokesman for the indigenous culture, the prevailing French influence in house decoration finally waned.

Chucho Reyes and other Mexican artists including Rufino Tamayo also explored Mexican themes in a manner reflecting pride in the indigenous traditions of their country.

The "yellow" living room of Chucho Reyes's house in Mexico City. The color emanates from the windows which Reyes painted yellow to give the effect of sunshine. A caricature of Reyes can be seen on the far table below the window. Above is the beam that divides the room into two perfect cubes.

Chucho Reyes

Jesús "Chucho" Reyes Ferreira (1880–1977) was an artist influential in resurrecting the traditional arts of Mexico. Born in Guadalajara, he inherited an interest in antiques from his antiquarian father. In 1913 he opened a shop in Guadalajara selling folk art and antiques, which he also began to amass into a considerable personal collection. He then became an artist, painting works full of the colors of Mexico and often reminiscent of Chagall.

Upon his arrival in Mexico City in 1938 Reyes became active in social circles, and often gave advice about interior decoration, steering his wealthy friends away from the prevailing French look and towards an aesthetic based on traditional Mexican elements, which he was able to assemble with a uniquely sophisticated eye.

His greatest influence, however, was on the emerging style of his close friend Luis Barragán. Often described as an inexhaustible source of ideas, Reyes was equally forthcoming with architectural advice. Blessed with an in-

stinct for proportion and obsessed with the Golden Mean, Reyes was often responsible for the height of a Barragán wall, or the placement of a Barragán window. During the 1940s, when Barragán was working on the gardens of Pedregal and his first Mexico City houses, Barragán paid Reyes by the day to act as his companion, assistant, and advisor. It was with Reyes's help that Barragán was able to apply so elegantly the lessons learned from visits to Mexico's old convents and haciendas, whose proportions and sense of solitude became the major influence in his subsequent and most important work.

Reyes's house, filled with memorabilia, antiques, and Mexican folk artifacts, was festive and chaotic. It was built around a courtyard with the living rooms on the upper floor, the rooms linked by the courtyard balcony. The living room was altered in size: the end wall was moved to make it into a perfect double cube, with a single wood beam delineation at the mid-point of the ceiling. The windows of the room were filled in, leaving

tiny square-shaped openings covered by hinged screens of wood similar to those found in convents. The glass was painted yellow so that the room is washed with yellow light, giving the effect of sunshine. The need to shut out the street, the grilled screens, and the yellow windows are all ideas which resurfaced later in the houses of Barragán.

Barragán and Reyes had a major falling out in the 1960s, Reyes claiming that Barragán failed to give him credit for his collaborations. The latter was later to redeem the situation somewhat with a posthumous tribute to Reyes in his address following his award of the Pritzker Prize in 1980: "Through his infallible aesthetic taste he was a great master in the difficult art of seeing with innocence. It pleases me . . . to recognize my debt to him for his profound lessons."

ABOVE: A cozy sitting
room on the upper level of the house is
filled with colonial paintings and a variety
of personal mementos. RIGHT: Another view
of the sitting room. Above the simple
fireplace is a snapshot of Reyes with his
adopted nephew.

Rufino Tamayo

Olga and Rufino Tamayo's house is in a pretty cobblestone alley in San Angel, hidden from the public gaze by the usual inscrutable wall. The Tamayo-designed house is unpretentious, and faces onto a large, rectangular herbaceous garden.

Rooms in the house are small in scale but rich in detail. There is a large studio upstairs where Tamayo, at the age of eighty-nine, still paints for three hours every day. A lifetime of collecting Mexican popular and pre-Hispanic art is much in evidence. Most of their enormous collection is now in museums, including the Rufino Tamayo Museum in Oaxaca, which Tamayo designed as a series of rooms, each one painted a different color. The *New York Times* once called it the world's most beautiful museum.

The Tamayos were among those who first worked to restore the popular and pre-Hispanic arts of Mexico to a position of national respect, and their house shows that their early joy in discovering these cultures is quite undiminished today.

Exotic and tropical vegetation surrounds the pathway leading to the house's main entrance.

146

TOP: The Tamayo garden is maintained under the watchful eye of Olga. Seen here is a Tamayo bronze sculpture and a pre-Columbian stone frog figure on a pedestal. MIDDLE: A vivid pre-Columbian terra-cotta child and traditional Mexican paper flowers, together with various other pre-Columbian and folkloric artifacts, decorate the coffee table. BOTTOM: A painted and lacquered hope chest of fragrant wood from the village of Olinala, in the state of Jalisco.

OVERLEAF LEFT: The dining room, with a recent painting by Tamayo. Olga Tamayo decorated the room in a simple, traditional Mexican manner. RIGHT: The stair landing is used to display Tamayo's extensive collection of pre-Columbian figures. The blue background was carefully chosen to show off the various rich shades of terra-cotta figures.

OLGA F. de TAMAYO

OPPOSITE: Standing against a roughly stuccoed wall, a bleached pine *trastero* (kitchen dresser) holds an assortment of Mexican folk art. ABOVE LEFT: Tamayo, at the age of eighty-nine, still paints for three hours every day in his spacious studio, which occupies half of the upper floor of the house. LEFT: This niche contains a display of Mexican candy skulls (sold during the Day of the Dead Festival) and other folkloric delicacies.

Frida Kahlo

Artist Frida Kahlo's remarkable life ended, as it also began, in the vivid blue house on the corner of Allende and Londres streets in Coyoacán, an old residential district in the south of Mexico City. In this attractive neighborhood of cobblestone streets and old colonial houses, conveniently close to the *zócalo* (main square) and market, Kahlo lived until her marriage at the age of twenty-two, to Diego Rivera. After periods spent in the United States and in the studios that Rivera built in nearby San Angel, Kahlo eventually returned to the house to live and work until her death in 1954.

Opposite: A magnificent pair of twelve-foot-high Judas figures frames the entrance. Beyond the entrance is a courtyard garden filled with tropical foliage. ABOVE RIGHT: A corner of the studio, overlooking the garden. On the desk is a faded drawing of Kahlo. RIGHT: The studio was designed for Kahlo by Diego Rivera.

At the age of eighteen a terrifying street-car accident left her with internal injuries and unable to bear children. The injuries necessitated more than thirty operations and long periods of hospitalization. Her marriage to Rivera was an emotional rollercoaster; Rivera's womanizing was an additional cross to bear. These traumatic events were a recurring autobiographical theme in her art, and she recorded with devastating candor her spirit and natural vivacity as well as her anguish at events beyond her control.

Her house was as much an outlet for her as were her paintings. After her death, Rivera gave the house, complete with its belongings, to the Mexican people. It now serves to perpetuate her memory, and over the lofty portal is the sign "Museo Frida Kahlo."

The house is painted *azul añil*, a deep matte blue traditionally used in Mexican houses to ward off evil spirits. Framing the portal are a pair of giant Judas figures, which are customarily filled with firecrackers and exploded on the festival of *Sabada de Gloria* (the Saturday before Easter), and symbolize both Judas and the betrayal of the people by

their oppressors (landowners, police, and politicians). After passing between these figures, one enters a courtyard garden filled with tropical foliage and trees, statues, and a stepped pyramid used as a pedestal for pre-Columbian idols.

The U-shaped house is fitted around the courtyard. French doors open into it from all sides, and were used for circulation in the absence of an internal corridor.

The room one initially enters is filled with a collection of paintings by Kahlo, Rivera, and artist friends such as Marcel Duchamp and Yves Tanguy. The nineteenth-century Mexican landscapist José Maria Velasco is also represented, as is Paul Klee. There

OPPOSITE: The house, now a museum, occupies the corner of an attractive cobblestone street in the old bohemian center of Coyoacán, near its *zócalo* (main square) and market. ABOVE: "Viva la Vida" (1954). This was Kahlo's last painting, executed shortly before she died.

is also a collection of colorful dresses from the isthmus of Tehuantepec. Frida, who was strikingly attractive, frequently caused a sensation during her visits to the U.S. by appearing in full native costume. Her collection of pre-Hispanic jewelry and terra cotta figurines from Teotihuacán and Tlatelcolco can also be seen. This was the living room, where the cosmopolitan Riveras entertained friends from around the world. The guest list included George Gershwin, Dolores del Rio, and Sergei Eisenstein; the exiled Trotsky, a neighbor, was also a frequent visitor.

Top: Hanging behind the dining room's French windows is a papier-mâché Judas figure (a favorite with Rivera) made by Carmen Caballero. The dressers display ceramics from Michoacán and glass from Tlaquepaque. MIDDLE: The kitchen was designed in the traditional manner by Kahlo. The straw *petate* on the floor is in the shape of a scorpion. BOTTOM: As in all traditional Mexican kitchens there is an array of miniature earthenware pots, in this case spelling "Frida" and "Diego," and next to this, a pair of doves tying a lover's knot. OPPOSITE: Above the yellow dining-room dresser is an anonymous Mexican still life. The masks are from Michoacán and were used for fiestas. Displayed on the dresser are pots from Tlaquepaque and ceramic animals from Ometepec.

Next to this was the dining room. There visitors were regaled by the family monkey and by Bonito the parrot, who performed tricks at the dining table and was rewarded with pats of butter. For this room Frida used masks and figures from various regions, including a large Day of the Dead skeleton, and household objects found in the local markets. As in peasant houses, the floor was painted with a bright yellow insect-repellant paint; a bare light bulb hung from the ceiling.

The adjacent kitchen, where Kahlo was often to be found working shoulder to shoulder with the kitchen staff, was remodeled with traditional blue, yellow, and white tiles. As in all true *Mexicanista* kitchens, there was an array of miniature earthenware mugs.

Next to the dining room, unexpectedly, is the master bedroom. Rivera was a man of unusual weight—over 300 pounds—with a corresponding appetite, and the bedroom's proximity to the kitchen can only, in the circumstances, have been felicitous.

In 1946 Rivera built a new

studio and bedroom wing of the local lava rock for Frida, who was becoming increasingly ill. Her bed was eventually moved to an alcove overlooking the garden for

OPPOSITE: The bed where Kahlo spent her last years was fitted with a mirror so that she could paint self-portraits. Above the bed is a portrait of a dead infant. The corset, which Kahlo customized with paint, speaks eloquently of her many illnesses. ABOVE: The guest bedroom, which was in later years occupied by the nurse. There is a record player, a dressing table, various anonymous paintings, and a portrait of Mao Tse-tung. LEFT: Another 1954 painting by Kahlo: "El Marxismo dará salud a los enfermos" (Marxism gives health to the sick).

160

LEFT: Rivera's bedroom, with his workclothes, jacket, and hat hanging on the wall. The handwoven curtain is from Michoacán. BELOW LEFT: On the wall in Rivera's bedroom is an anonymous battle scene; over the bed is a 1938 photo of Kahlo. The pillows are hand-embroidered and the bedspread is hand-crocheted. OPPOSITE: On a side table in the guest bedroom stands a lacquered box from Olinala and a photograph of Diego Rivera holding his pet monkey. Above it is a glass-fronted cabinet full of folk objects.

her final years so she could watch the trees, the pigeons, and the changing light.

The influence of the Kahlo house can still be seen in many Mexican houses today. Even the most wealthy have a wide range of cultured artifacts, past and present, from Mexico's Indian heritage, displayed proudly alongside the colonial antiques, and contemporary Italian furniture.

José Luis Cuevas

José Luis Cuevas, born in 1934, lives in a house built for him in San Angel in 1970 by architects Abraham Zabludowsky and Teodoro Gonzalez de León. Cuevas is a leading Mexican artist, successful from a very early age: he had his first one-man show in Mexico City at the age of nineteen. His studio occupies the upper level of the house and is dominated by a huge nineteenth-century brass bed that is surrounded by religious paintings, two original *Vanity Fair* caricatures by Miguel Covarrubias, and a collection of antiques and fetishistic objects.

Cuevas became seriously ill in the mid-1970s and spent the illness in his brass bed, thinking that if he should die this is where he wanted to be. Much of the collection around the bed was given to him by friends during his illness, including a sand-clock from Chucho Reyes. The flow of sand stopped and in doing so, Cuevas claims, stopped his death.

Top: The studio is dominated by an ornate brass bed which was installed during Cuevas's serious illness in the 1970s. Surrounding it are gifts brought by his friends during this period. ABOVE: The studio occupies the entire upper floor of the house. It is filled with an eclectic array of furniture, artifacts, books, and art with which Cuevas likes to surround himself while working. OPPOSITE: Next to Cuevas's bed is a collection of *retablos,* mementos, and a Covarrubias caricature painted for *Vanity Fair* in the 1930s.

CHAPTER SIX

THE HOUSES OF LUIS BARRAGAN

L uis Barragán was born in Guadalajara in 1902 of a prosperous, aristocratic family, and grew up on a large ranch near the remote village of Mazamitla in Michoacán, a region known for its beautiful vernacular architecture.

Although trained as an engineer, Barragán discovered he had a closer affinity with architecture. He did not receive formal training and never officially became an architect (which did not prevent him from receiving the Pritzker Award, architecture's "Nobel Prize," in 1980). His architectural education came from engineering school (which was sufficient to enable him to build houses), from other architects, and from practical experience. He felt later that his lack of academic training in architecture was probably a blessing—freeing him from the rigid approach of many of his peers and allowing him to arrive at instinctive solutions to design problems.

In his early twenties Barragán spent a formative two years in Europe. In France he encountered the writings of Ferdinand Bac, a French landscape architect, illustrator, and intellectual. Bac's illustrated books on the art of landscaping—*Le Colombier* and *The Enchanted Gardens*—suggested that gardens should be enchanted places for meditation, with the capacity to "bewitch" the onlooker. These ideas were a huge influence on Barragán's future landscaping career, especially since he was able to relate the Mediterranean environment portrayed in Bac's illustrations to his native Guadalajara

165

O PPOSITE: Casa Galvez (1955). A small sitting room overlooks an exterior pool and fountain. The colored wall surrounding the pool is designed to visually become a fourth wall of the room, creating a combined indoor and outdoor space.

T OP: Barragán was inspired by the colonial convents, monasteries, and haciendas of Mexico, such as the interior of this ex-convent in Puebla. The juxtaposition of door opening and window on the right prefigures similar Barragán compositions. ABOVE: The *trojes* (granaries) of Mexico's haciendas appealed most of all to Barragán. The simplicity, proportion, and monumentality of the granary in the hacienda of Tenexac combine in the kind of space often described today as being "very Barragán-like."

with its similar climate. When Barragán finally met Bac and discussed architecture with him, Bac showed him "with the force of a revelation" a new and deeper understanding of the basic elements of building: beams, roof-tiles, arches, and how natural elements such as rocks and stones, the water, and the horizon played a role in design.

Returning to Guadalajara, Barragán resumed a friendship with two architects of his generation, Rafael Urzua and Ignacio Díaz Morales. They were also beginning to build houses with a Moroccan influence similar to those of Barragán. Together they studied the Bac books, and Barragán began to design patios which would "bewitch" the user, and to pursue his search for an "emotional architecture."

In the late 1930s Barragán moved to Mexico City. He designed a series of buildings in the International Style, which by then had become popular in Mexico (more so than in almost any other country).

It was in the 1940s that Barragán began to discover the more personal style by which his later mature work is so easily recognized. From 1943 to 1950 he was occupied with the gardens of Pedregal, a landscaping project in a wilderness area of black volcanic outcrops near San Angel in the southern part of Mexico City. His intention was to create an area of select housing, disturbing as little as possible the unusual, almost lunar landscape. He acted as developer and architect, designing several houses for the Pedregal and laying out streets, pools, pathways, and fountains—always in a manner that deferred to the natural rock formations. Walls of lava-rock divided individual lots; natural vegetation, augmented by cacti and pepper-trees, was preserved.

Soon after Barragán moved to Mexico City he had met another Guadalajaran, Chucho Reyes. Reyes—an artist, antiquarian, and taste-maker (his own house is included elsewhere in this book) was a passionate advocate of the indigenous culture of Mexico. He had been influential in the transition from French to Mexican influences in interior decoration which occurred during the 1930s and 1940s. A strong affinity developed between the two men, and Reyes soon became a major influence in Barragán's creative growth.

During the period of his work on the Pedregal, Barragán employed Reyes (paying him by the day) as a consultant. In addition to helping

with everyday design problems, Reyes was a catalyst in Barragán's radical metamorphosis of style. Barragán's generic, International-Style apartment buildings and Moroccan-influenced houses of the 1930s gave way to the highly abstract and personal work of his mature period, beginning in the 1940s with the Pedregal and continuing as a process of refinement for the remainder of his career.

During this period of transformation, Barragán discovered his country. His subsequent architecture can be seen as a distillation of the proportions and details of old Mexican colonial convents, monasteries, and haciendas. A profound Catholic, Barragán was also influenced by the spirit of grace and solitude with which these buildings are strongly imbued.

At the same time, a number of Barragán's most characteristic decorative motifs began to make their appearance. These included the groupings of giant *pulque* fermenting pots on the patio of his later houses, and the use of colored, mirrored balls which had originally hung inside nineteenth-century *pulquerias* (liquor stores). They appeared in symbolic clusters on Barragán's coffee tables. Barragán's palette, which had hitherto been limited to Indian red, blue, and off-white, suddenly adopted the vibrant hues of Mexican traditional clothing and festivals: yellows, pinks, reds, and purples. These design decisions were all influenced by Chucho Reyes.

During the 1950s and thereafter, Barragán became involved in more landscaping and residential planning projects. He built a chapel in 1955 at Tlalpan in Mexico City, and designed others which remained unbuilt.

Barragán was never prolific, but it is nonetheless disappointing that during the period encompassing the last thirty years of his active life he produced only three houses: Casa Galvez in the 1950s, San Cristóbal in the 1960s, and Casa Gilardi in the 1970s.

Partly because very little of his equally remarkable landscaping work has survived, Barragán is best known for his houses. Each house was a variation on a continuing theme. Barragán was uninterested in technical innovation, and was content with a simple vocabulary of materials, such as adobe and timber beams.

His houses were monastic in spirit and provided a refuge from

Top: Casa Farah (1936), by Rafael Urzua, a close friend of Barragán; he also worked in Guadalajara during the 1920s and 1930s in a similar Morocco-inspired vein. MIDDLE: This detail of a balustrade at Casa Farah shows the blue also used by Barragán at this time. BOTTOM: One of Barragán's first houses, built in Guadalajara in 1930.

Top: One of a series of International-Style apartments built by Barragán in the late 1930s; this one is near the center of Mexico City. ABOVE: The elegant International-Style Parque Hippodromo duplex in Mexico City (1938). The top floor was designed as a solarium, with bedrooms and living room on the third and second floors, respectively, and a garage on the ground floor. OPPOSITE: A view from the garden at Casa Luna, showing a small, square pool with a fountain in the center. The water cascades gently into another pool at the garden level below. Inspired by the Alhambra Gardens in Spain, it is covered by an arched pavilion. The main house is seen through the arch.

contemporary life. The closely integrated interior and exterior spaces were surrounded by walls designed to create a private and serene environment. Window sizes were limited except when facing a private courtyard, with its pool and fountain. As Barragán explained: "Architecture, besides being spatial, is also musical. That music is played with water. The importance of walls is that they isolate one from the street's exterior space. The street is aggressive, even hostile: walls create silence. From that silence you can play with water as music. Afterwards, that music surrounds us."

The wall is the most Mexican of building elements, and with Barragán it received new expression, becoming a sculpture and achieving an extraordinary plasticity and monumentality. Doors, windows, and other interruptions of the wall surface were placed with the utmost deliberation. Barragán was constantly making changes during construction, often pulling a wall down and starting again.

He used walls to create an all-enveloping domestic enclosure, allowing glimpses of the sky but little else of the outside world. Views focused instead on the patio, which was itself surrounded by high walls. His complaint with most modern houses was their profusion of windows which allowed indiscriminate views of the outside world and competed for the occupant's attention. In Barragán's houses the interior is cozy, protective, and without distraction.

Barragán placed walls in a way that orchestrated a systematic "unveiling" of the interior as the visitor entered the house and progressed from space to space. His intention was theatrical; it provided what he liked to refer to as an "architectural striptease."

Color was used on wall surfaces for spatial effect or to express moods. A wall might be painted blue as a metaphor for the sky, or yellow to give an effect of sunlight.

In the address he gave on receiving the Pritzker Award, he gave an indication of the importance he placed on the intangibles of architecture: "In alarming proportions the following words have disappeared from architectural publications: beauty, inspiration, magic, sorcery, enchantment, and also serenity, mystery, silence, privacy, astonishment. All of these have found a loving home in my soul."

Casa Luna

In 1930, at the age of twenty-eight, Barragán designed a family house in Guadalajara for Efraim Gonzalez Luna, a lawyer, political leader, intellectual, and writer. Luna translated French classics into Spanish, and was one of the founders of the National Action Party. The house, which is still owned by the family, is lively and romantic, a sense of mystery and magic (inspired perhaps by Ferdinand Bac), pervading its trellis-covered terraces and pools.

The exterior is distinguished by a variety of small openings, suggesting a Moroccan influence and pointing the way to a similar massiveness in Barragán's later work. This North African-Islamic treatment is shared by other houses in the same neighborhood built by Rafael Urzua and Ignacio Díaz Morales.

The interior is solidly built and carefully detailed. There is a foretaste of Barragán's later work in the simple detailing of bookshelves, the reading stand in the large upstairs

Opposite: The carefully detailed stair balustrade, showing the blue edging, one of three colors used by Barragán during this period. ABOVE: The extensive library (the owner was an intellectual, lawyer, and politico). LEFT: The library's reading stand, similar to those in colonial convents.

library (recalling those in colonial monasteries), and in the sequence of spaces through the house. These alternate between high and low, ample and narrow, generating surprise and emotion. The stairs are sculptural and are built around a study recess. A vivid blue is used unexpectedly in the balustrade detailing.

A rear patio is enlivened by a small, square pool and fountain. The pool is surrounded on three sides by a wooden balustrade, and shaded by an overhead pergola. The water falls in a miniature cascade to another pool below.

LEFT: The *sala* shows Casa Luna's Moorish influence. The house still has many of its original furnishings. ABOVE: The Moorish influence is also evident in the strong massing and the variety of shapes in the openings of the exterior.

Casa Prieto

Casa Prieto was the first house built by Barragán on his Pedregal project, in 1943. The original owners, Eduardo and Tella Prieto, still occupy the house and recall Barragán in the 1940s as a charming and persuasive salesman. First, he sold them the land, then the idea of building the house—which, as a young couple, they could not really afford. When it finally took shape, the house was much bigger (and far more expensive) than the Prietos had ever imagined, and they had to sell everything, even their car, to pay for it.

Externally, the strongest feature is the entry courtyard, an elegant square space with plain walls of white and brilliant yellow. They are the first manifestations of the abstract, minimalist approach that marked Barragán's later work.

A small vestibule leads into a reception area at once impressive and unexpected. Set at a lower level than the living area beyond, it shares the same lofty, wood-beamed roof which extends to the left in dramatic perspective over the living area. To the right is

OPPOSITE: The choice of furniture and artifacts in this corner of the *sala* is characteristic of Barragán. On the Barragán-designed dresser is a lamp (also by Barragán) with a parchment shade, a mirrored ball, and a Goeritz gold-leaf painting. ABOVE: Steps lead from the entry lobby up to the dining room. The door is hinged in the middle and doubles as a screen. The mirrored balls, often seen in Barragán interiors, come from nineteenth-century *pulquerias*.

LEFT: The lofty entry lobby, its space reminiscent of hacienda granaries, has steps leading up to the main *sala* and down to the bedrooms. Presiding over the space is a Goeritz statue of a winged angel. ABOVE: A view from the *sala* over a low balustrade toward the circulation area, the Goeritz winged angel, and a passage through to other living areas.

the dining room, screened from the reception area by a wall placed so that too much is not revealed too soon. This is an example of Barragán's concept of "visual striptease," although in this particular case it was his advisor, Chucho Reyes, who suggested adding the wall that had not been on the original plans.

One flight of steps leads up to the living room, while another leads up to the dining room, penetrating the screen wall with a square-shaped door, split into two vertical leaves, like a screen.

Despite its size, the living room is not imposing. The furniture is simple and in harmony with the architecture. There are selective views of the garden through carefully placed windows. Beside the fireplace is a landscape of a Mexican pueblo by Dr. Atl, one of the artists who, in the early 1920s, pioneered the cultural movement to recognize Mexico's indigenous art and architecture. The Prietos also have a large collection of paintings by their friend Chucho Reyes.

The garden is surrounded by high walls covered with vines and hidden by trees. The original lot was much larger, but much of it was sold off to family members.

The Pedregal was a surreal landscape of black lava beds when Casa Prieto was built. In Barragán's plans, the lava beds interacted with widely spaced houses and careful landscaping. The Pedregal is now a conventional, if exclusive, suburb. All Barragán's original lots have been divided up, and much of the lava has disappeared as if it never existed.

OPPOSITE TOP: The entry courtyard. This is the first example of the abstract, minimalist treatment of walls characteristic of Barragán's mature work. BOTTOM: The first example of Barragán's signature grouping of *pulque* pots (however, a similar grouping already existed in his collaborator's, Chucho Reyes, own kitchen courtyard).

San Cristóbal

Barragán's lifelong affinity with the horse is expressed in his 1967 design for the Folke Egerström family. The San Cristóbal complex includes a family house, swimming pool, and stables. The Egerströms breed thoroughbred race-horses, and the stables were designed to be an environment in which one could enjoy the aesthetics of the horse.

The focus of the stables is a plazalike space, edged by a composition of brilliantly colored walls that provide a backdrop for the animals as they are paraded past. Carefully edited gaps in the walls reveal glimpses of a surrounding landscape into which the horses eventually disappear to continue their exercises. A large pool, one side of the house, and box stalls further anchor the composition.

San Cristóbal is a one-hour drive north from Mexico City on the Querétaro highway. On leaving the city, the highway passes the famous Satellite Towers, a monument to the suburb of Ciudad Satellite. Barragán designed this in 1957 with the collaboration of artist Mathias Goeritz.

Besides its thoroughbred horses, San Cristóbal is home to a variety of other animals. OPPOSITE: San Cristóbal is a stunning reinterpretation of a traditional farm. The constant cascade of water emerges from a sloping chute sandwiched between two lofty and closely spaced walls.

Architecture as *mise-en-scène*. From this vantage point at the shallow-sloping edge of the pond, and sheltered by the stable roof, one awaits the daily parade of horses against the backdrop of a perfectly scaled wall. To complete a perfect composition: the cascade to the left and the tree to the right.

San Cristóbal is in the residential subdivision of Los Clubes, which Barragán designed between 1964 and 1965. It is entered through a high, typically Barragán gateway next to an often-photographed fountain (known as the Lovers' Fountain), which is now in a sad state of neglect.

A long, straight driveway leads from the entry gates to the stables compound. The visitor's anticipation in catching a glimpse of the stables is quickly rewarded, but only slightly. As usual, Barragán, with his sense of theater, reveals only a little at a time. The white-painted house, conservative by Barragán standards and evidently designed to offer no visual competition to the stables, is to the left of the driveway, and commands no more than a glance. The stables at this point already attract total attention, though only a flash of tree and water are visible through a gap in a vividly colored wall stretching across the landscape.

The compound is reached via a processional route which skirts around the pond. A cascade of water descends into the pond from between the ends of what is now revealed as a double wall—the wall which is first visible on entering the property. Next to the pond is a large stereotypical tree beneath which families of geese fuss over eggs and offspring. A long *corredor* (or covered porch) gives shelter to the box stalls, and provides a vantage point, complete with benches and tables, for viewing one of the twentieth century's most remarkable and poetic spaces.

At one's feet, the cobbled floor slopes imperceptibly into the water. Beyond the pool is the perimeter wall, at a scale that provides the perfect backdrop for the horses. As the horses are paraded past, seemingly larger than life, they become actors in an immaculately orchestrated daily ritual.

One's initial view the stable compound from the farm's entrance pathway. OVERLEAF: The stable's *corredor* is ruled by a concierge-like turkey. The pond is beyond the *corredor*, to the right.

Casa Galvez

Luis Barragán built this house for Antonio and Emilia Galvez and their seven children in 1955, just after he finished the Tlalpan chapel. It is in Mexico City, on a quiet cobbled street in Chimalistac, near San Angel. A massive timber door sheltered by a pink portico opens onto a small courtyard paved in black volcanic rock and furnished with a long bench and a cluster of *pulque* pots.

Barragán designed the house (including the garden, wall colors, furniture, and upholstery) in its entirety, and little has changed since it was new. The L-shaped house, formed of two rectangular units, is surrounded by a large terrace. Behind the terrace is a simple garden, divided into separate, interconnecting spaces by massive plantings and subtly placed steps.

The interior has the quality of an elaborate abstract composition. Architecture is reduced to broad, intersecting wall planes which unfold as one penetrates gradually into the inner sanctum, and finally

OPPOSITE: The simple entry doors of Casa Galvez. ABOVE: Barragán's landscaping is subtle. A large clump of jasmine divides the areas, and narrow, concrete steps allow the grass surface to continue up to the edge of the drop.

faces the huge windows opening onto the massively scaled rear terrace and garden. White wall and ceiling surfaces are punctuated intermittently by a pink wall or an ocher ceiling. One side of a small sitting room is entirely glazed. Beyond the glass is an exterior pool, surrounded by a pink wall which becomes the fourth wall of the room. It also acts as a sounding board for the fountain, filling the room with the delicate splash of running water.

Furnishings are simple and comfortable. Couches and chairs are upholstered in handwoven cotton. Tables, cabinets, and built-in furniture are formed of simple slabs of bleached wood. There are a number of paintings in vivid Mexican colors by Pedro Coronel, and a famous Diego Rivera nude, "Nieves."

The house has existed for years, but still looks new. It is maintained under the careful eye of Emilia Galvez and her daughter Cristina (director of the Rufino Tamayo Museum), who still live in the house.

OPPOSITE: The front patio, with a reflecting pool and fountain enclosed by a high wall. Next to the pool is a small sitting room (shown on page 164). Behind the *pulque* pots from Michoacán is the covered entry lobby. ABOVE: The sitting room, with its corner fireplace (Barragán disliked symmetry and often butted windows, pictures, or fireplaces up to a room's corner). The design of *butacas* (the classic armchair of Mexico) was simplified by Barragán; these have a frame of *sabino* (a signature Barragán wood) and stretched cowhide. They are grouped around a simple coffee table resting on *petates*. The cabinet to the left is faced with square lattice (another Barragán motif).

ABOVE: The dining room, with a 1960 Pedro Coronel painting. The lamp, console table, and dining table are by Barragán; the chairs are from Taxco. The fruit rests on traditional Mexican tissue paper. LEFT: Distinctive doors open to a sitting room and the dining room; both rooms have paintings by Coronel. OPPOSITE: Barragán deliberately placed this Goeritz gold-leaf painting at the junction of two walls, echoing compositions like those in the convent on page 166. The stairs are of volcanic stone.

The study, with a Barragán reading stand and "Nieves," a magnificent Diego Rivera painting of an Indian girl arranging calla lilies.

Casa Gilardi

The Gilardi House, designed and built in the late 1970s, was the last house designed by Barragán. The owner, Francisco Gilardi, is a young, successful businessman involved in the world of television and advertising. An admirer of Barragán, he went to see him without an introduction. Barragán had not designed a house for several years and had to be persuaded to visit the 10-by-30-meter site not far from his office near Chapultepec Park in the center of Mexico City. When Barragán agreed, it was on one simple condition: the large jacaranda tree in the middle of the site must be kept, and the house built around it.

Behind a perfectly square façade of Mexican-pink stucco, the house reveals itself stage by stage. Progression through the house is orchestrated in a masterful (and almost theatrical) manner, manipulated by a controlled use of natural light and color to create particular effects. A simple vestibule leads to a larger reception hall where a staircase begins its ascent to the more private reaches of

A BOVE: The house was built around a mature jacaranda. The yellow-painted windows of the passage to the dining room and swimming pool are seen at bottom right. RIGHT: The bright but inscrutable façade of Casa Gilardi faces a busy semicommercial street in Tacubaya, Mexico City.

194

the house. This is lit softly from a rooflight high above. Beyond this is a long, white-painted passage, unlit and dark as it passes the kitchen, then washed by light from a series of yellow-painted vertical strip windows. This yellow light, filtering in from the courtyard, gives a sunny feeling even on dull days, and acts as a prelude to the house's principal drama.

At the end of this passage, doors open to reveal the pool room, with its end wall of vivid blue. This room—containing only the swimming pool, a dining table, chairs, and a low bench—is used for entertaining clients and friends. Except when its surface is disturbed during swimming, the pool is as still as glass. The blue section of the back wall corresponds to a recessed skylight above and gives the effect of pulling the sky down into the water. The emptiness of the room reflects Barragán's love of monastic spaces and his metaphysical preoccupation with solitude.

The dining table faces onto the courtyard and the jacaranda tree. When the tree blossoms during April, it carpets the volcanic-stone paving with purple flowers. The other private living quarters occupy the upper floors of the front section of the house. A relatively conventional living room opens onto a small patio which would overlook the street except that the walls have been made so high that only the sky is visible. Barragán's city patios all share this characteristic of not letting the city intrude. On the patio there is an arrangement of clay *pulque* pots, another familiar element of Barragán's architecture.

The house was created on a limited budget, and on a difficult urban lot backed by houses on three sides. Barragán not only kept the jacaranda tree and integrated it into the overall design, he also gave his client a remarkable work of art.

Opposite: The sculptural staircase is lit by a skylight high above.

Overleaf, TOP LEFT: The dining table in the pool room, with a bowl of Mexican fruit. BOTTOM LEFT: The walls of the passage are painted white, but the glass of the vertical windows is coated with yellow paint. Beyond is the pool room. RIGHT: A corner of the pool room, with its rose-red sculptural column.

CHAPTER SEVEN

THE CONTINUING TRADITION

Even after his death, a giant figure continues to dominate Mexican architecture. That figure is Luis Barragán.

The influential phase of Barragán's work began in the mid-1940s, after a decade of involvement with the International Style. In the years that followed—and with the help of artist Chucho Reyes—he evolved a new design vocabulary based on a distillation of elements borrowed from colonial haciendas and convents and mixed with the indigenous colors of Mexico.

The International Style had been heralded throughout the 1920s by the architectural theorist José Villagrán Garcia, who had studied the work of Gropius and Le Corbusier. The Style arrived in Mexico in 1930, with the completion of Diego Rivera's studio in San Angel, built by architect Juan O'Gorman and reached its zenith in the 1950s. Mario Pani, Max Cetto, Juan Sordo Madaleno, Victor de la Lama, and others built houses of great sophistication, often with glass curtain walls in the manner of Mies van der Rohe. Mies himself spent time in Mexico in the early 1950s, staying with Enrique del Moral, an architect whose style was closer to that of Barragán. Richard Neutra,

OPPOSITE: A monastic staircase at the Ortiz Monasterio house leads up to the master bedroom, turning sharply to the right. Then an associate of Barragán's, architect Andrés Casillas was inspired by the staircase in Barragán's own house in Mexico City.

A simple wall in a new, architect-designed house in Valle de Bravo illustrates the sense of color and innocence still prevalent in Mexican design.

an American architect who was a friend of Barragán, wrote in 1952: "Mexico is the most vital country of the Americas. Here the most modern innovations in architecture and the arts are married to indigenous trends of an indigenous people."

By the 1950s many Mexican architects had become disenchanted with the sterility of the International Style and its lack of reference to Mexico. At this point they fell under the benign influence of Barragán, who had found the perfect formula for a Mexican architecture.

Today, Barragán's architecture has created a compelling national vernacular from which few architects have chosen to deviate. Barragán's influence extends to nearly every detail of furniture and ornamentation. His distinctive chairs, tables, and built-in shelves and cabinets—as well as the cluster of *pulque* pots on the patio and the bowl of mirrored balls on the overscaled coffee table—all these are part of the Barragán "kit" of design elements. Their virtue is that they are all distinctively Mexican, and thus continue a tradition of nationalistic influences on domestic design that began after the Revolution ended in 1920.

The unwillingness of contemporary architects to take a decisive leap past this legacy is due to several factors. Among these is Mexico's fervent nationalism (well shown by a decision by Francisco Toledo, one of the country's most important living artists, never to exhibit outside Mexico) and corresponding isolation from new international influences and trends. In addition, the lack of any architectural media prevents any real forum to promote change, and the usual peer pressure to be published, which has become an undeniable influence on the rapid growth of new aesthetics elsewhere, does not exist. One hopes that when the leap does eventually occur it will still show an indebtedness to Barragán and also retain the three magic elements of Mexican architecture: the wall, the courtyard, and the bold use of color.

Yet while contemporary Mexican residential design may lack a radical spirit, there is still much to admire—not least the underrated quality of liveability. Barragán had advocated that a house be an oasis, a refuge of calm and intimacy in an increasingly hostile world. His architecture, while having these characteristics, was also essentially monastic in spirit.

In place of his austerity, today's architects provide a softer and richer environment. Natural materials—wood, adobe, stone, and local tile—are used as well as muted colors in which earth tones predominate; the vivid hues favored by Barragán are less evident. Strategically placed skylights, often hidden behind roof beams and lattices, cast patterned shadows. Scale is generous; doors, bookshelves, tables, and other furniture are often formed of huge slabs of wood, giving a feeling of both simplicity and luxury. Frequent level changes are anchored by broad, low, wide stuccoed balustrades. Spaces are orchestrated as one progresses through the house, in turn dramatic and intimate.

In these houses there is also evidence of the availability of cheap labor. (Surprisingly, it is cheaper to build a stuccoed wall than to use a prefabricated one.) Everywhere the "handmade" look is evident, in contrast to the more machined and impersonal finish prevalent in the United States and in Europe.

Top: Stairs lead dramatically up from an interior courtyard to the bedroom level of this 1989 house by Ricardo Legorreta. ABOVE: The opposite end of the same courtyard is planted with a tree and is overlooked by a caged balcony, simultaneously suggesting a stage set and a traditional colonial courtyard (or its Moorish antecedent—one expects a veiled woman to appear behind the bars).

Casa
Ortiz Monasterio

Surrounded by pine-covered mountains, the picturesque colonial town of Valle de Bravo is set at the side of a large lake. It is a popular weekend resort for sports-loving Mexico City residents, and it is an important waterskiing center. It is also the location of the Ortiz Monasterio house, designed in 1970 by Andrés Casillas—an architect who once worked with Barragán, in particular on the design of San Cristóbal.

The house is set beneath La Peña—a huge rock which dominates the town—and enjoys spectacular views of the lake. The entry path winds through a rock garden, ending in a patio. The living room has a large picture window and a staircase, reminiscent of the one in Barragán's own 1947 house, which seems to disappear into a slot in the rear wall, turns, and continues up to the master bedroom.

Tᴏᴘ: The chimneys form a rhythm that repeats the slope of the hillside. ᴀʙᴏᴠᴇ: A cavern encountered on the pathway up to the house. ᴏᴘᴘᴏsɪᴛᴇ: The view from the pathway, which winds between the rocks. The crags of La Peña are echoed in the strongly sculptured forms of the house.

Casa Gomez

The house was designed for Carlos Gomez and his family in the early 1980s by architect Ricardo Legorreta, Mexico's best-known living architect. The house is large and has a slanting tiled roof—a radical departure for Legorreta who until then had always utilized Barragánesque flat roofs to preserve a rectilinear geometry. (When he told Barragán "You won't believe this, but I'm thinking of doing a sloping roof," Barragán is said to have replied "How daring you are!")

The house is designed with a row of balconies overlooking a swimming pool. The pool is contained within a high wall and glimpsed from the rest of the garden through the square perforations of a large gate. The squared grillwork is a familiar motif in the work of Barragán, Legorreta, and other Mexican architects, and is of Moorish origins.

The house has large, comfortable living areas furnished with contemporary Mexican furniture, some antiques, and a collection of paintings, in-

cluding a Botero nun. Each bedroom has a private balcony which overlooks both the pool and a fine view. The principal bathroom is lit by skylights and is large enough to be mistaken for an extra living room.

ABOVE: The pool is enclosed by a high wall and glimpsed through the square perforations of a large gate. LEFT: The entry courtyard is an attractive re-creation of a traditional Mexican space. OPPOSITE: A nun by Fernando Botero overlooks a table and contemporary Mexican chairs.

Looking more like a living room than the bathroom it is, this space is lit lavishly from overhead, with the light diffused by beams.

Casa Cervantes

The Cervantes house was designed by Ricardo Legorreta for his daughter, Lucia, and her family. The house is built on the edge of a steep ravine so that most of the house is well below the street. The main living areas are on the lowest levels. A patio outside the living areas stretches the width of the house, and has steps leading down to a narrow garden.

Both the exterior and the interior of the house are painted white with particular walls defined by bright graphic colors. The house faces south and is filled with light all day.

Legorreta, who is best known for his Camino Real hotels and other commercial projects, considers himself to be "an architect of the people," using familiar motifs in often playful ways to evoke a positive response from the man in the street. This design philosophy contrasts with Barragán's monasticism and is well portrayed in the design of this and other recent houses in Mexico City.

ABOVE: Color and form are used to delineate design elements of the garden façade, preventing what would otherwise be a bland, flat expanse of wall. RIGHT: The stable-door window, first used in Mexico by the conquistadores, was used several times by Barragán. In this bedroom it is used for its ability to control the amount of light and fresh air that can be let in. The attractive use of color used throughout the house continues in this room. OPPOSITE: The living room and dining room are defined by a strong use of color. The dado is taken from similar painted surfaces in primitive buildings.

Mexico City Residence

This house is by Juan Sordo Madaleno, a contemporary of Barragán. Responsible for a large number of important commercial and residential projects during his successful career, he died several years ago.

In this house, typical of his later work, there are echoes of Barragán, but Madaleno's approach to design was formed independently (although he and Barragán did share friendship with the influential Chucho Reyes).

The house presents the usual blank wall to the street. Entering, one emerges into a large courtyard dominated by a metal Christ figure by Mathias Goeritz and a long, narrow pool, which resembles the horse troughs found in rural haciendas.

The interior of the house offers a series of dramatic spatial transitions. One is the transition from the low entry vestibule to a lobby lit by a skylight twenty-five feet above. Passing up a shallow flight of steps to the living areas, the flow of space be-

comes horizontal. Here, furniture and artifacts are arranged in bold groupings that accentuate the simplicity of materials and the rectilinear design of the architecture.

OPPOSITE: To the left of this lobby is a low entry vestibule. TOP: The elegant dining room, with furniture designed by the architect. ABOVE: The entry courtyard.

Casa Yturbe

The house designed by José de Yturbe for his wife, Malena, and their family is in Lomas, on the west side of Mexico City. A discreet door in the high, protective street wall admits the visitor to a flight of steps which leads down and around a corner to a patio covered with terra-cotta paving. One side of the patio is a sheltered seating area with a pool and fountain, landscaped with tropical foliage.

The house is entered through a small doorway flanked by plants and a large urn which was originally used to bring olive oil from Spain to America. Low, stuccoed balustrades with the curved edges that appear everywhere in Yturbe's work (and that are inspired by the traditional stuccoed walls in old haciendas) flank the entry space. This space is brightly lit by skylights overhead, giving it a welcoming ambience.

Within the house the furnishings have been kept simple, comfortable, and Mexican. Most of the furniture was designed by Yturbe, while his wife Malena designed armchairs and lamps. There are ceramics by the Mexican potter Gorky and paintings by several Mexican artists. There is a large, cozy library with shelves designed in generous wood sections by Yturbe. Earth and wood colors predominate throughout the house, and as with all Yturbe's work, the feeling is one of simplicity and homogeneity.

ABOVE: The library bookshelves are framed in the familiar Mexican square grid. The furniture is by Malena Yturbe, the architect's wife. OPPOSITE: The large urn in the entry courtyard was originally used to bring olive oil from Spain to America.

214

Lakeshore Retreat

Architect José de Yturbe's own weekend house at Valle de Bravo is built on the edge of the lake. A comfortable family house, it is constructed of adobe-covered masonry walls and roughly carved pine columns supporting the tiled roof typical of the area. The climate is mild all year round, and the house follows a familiar Valle pattern, with an outdoor living terrace facing the view, as well as enclosed living areas which give more protection during the rainy season. The interior living space is large, and it is separated from the dining area by a low, stuccoed balustrade and a change of level in the tiled floor.

The most important space is the terrace, which is used most of the year and is equally popular by day or by night, when the large fireplace helps offset the lakeside chill. The large built-in coffee table is covered in white-painted stucco. Other furniture is also built-in, and there are additional *equipal* chairs.

Top: The house faces the lake and is becoming enveloped in tropical foliage. ABOVE: The terrace, where the family spends most of its time. OPPOSITE: A corner of the living room. The cupboard with marquetry edging is by Malena Yturbe, wife of the architect.

Overleaf: Like a silent audience awaiting the dinner party, row after row of geraniums are lit by a skylight. Yturbe designed the dining table and chairs; the ceramics are by Gorky, a well-known potter from Guanajuaro.

Manolo Mestre, Architect

Mestre has an unusually broad knowledge and love of Mexican indigenous and colonial architecture, and this particular involvement shows itself in his busy architectural practice. Mestre's houses are characterized as much as anything by memorable, individual spaces, often reflecting architectural details and spaces he has seen on his travels—the twist of a staircase, or the way that sunlight falls from a concealed skylight through wood slats (or simple cut branches), making simple patterns on a color-washed wall. Each of his houses is distinguished by felicitous "moments" such as these. They are also comfortable and well planned: his clients need a house in which they can relax with their families after a busy week at the office.

OPPOSITE: Mestre achieves a charming effect through his use of simple materials, color, and a strategically placed skylight. The stairs lead from the entry lobby to the bedroom. ABOVE: A Mestre entry lobby. A traditional wood trellis conceals a glass skylight. RIGHT: Beyond and below this low, stuccoed balustrade is the living room.

ALONG THE COAST

T he climatic contrast between Mexico's high-altitude cities on the Central Plateau and the coastal resorts which line the Pacific Coast is dramatic. A quick thirty-minute flight on Mexicana transports the modern traveler from a cool, temperate environment to one of tropical humidity and a landscape of palms, jungle, and thatched *palapa* roofs.

223

Mexico is blessed with over 2,000 miles of Pacific coastline, with an endless variety of rocky headlands and sandy beaches sweeping in a lazy curve from Baja California in the Northwest to Chiapas in the Southeast, where the landscape is fully tropical.

In this southern coastal region, architecture appears to have undergone a melting process. Profiles are softer, and the usual definition between the interior and the exterior becomes blurred. No longer needed as room enclosures, except to provide privacy and spatial definition, walls have seemingly unwrapped themselves from their usual rigid positions. They float off beyond the confines of interior space, dissolving gently into the landscaping, leading the eye outward to the ocean view. Angles have been replaced by sensuous curves, whether defining the edges of a stuccoed banquette, or low, molded balustrades which punctuate changes of level. Overhead, the voluminous *palapa* roof is draped softly over columns formed from palm trees, giving both a lofty interior space and a low, protective eave.

O PPOSITE: An idyllic view of Costa Careyes from a *casita*, owned by Giorgio Brignone, beside the harbor. In the foreground is a small swimming pool.

Aᴮᴼᵛᴱ: A corner of the living room in Casa Talec. A large *palapa* roof is supported by a palm trunk embraced by an *amate* vine. ᴼᴾᴾᴼˢᴵᵀᴱ: The roof terrace of Gian Franco Brignone's house on the edge of a cliff in Costa Careyes.

Houses of this kind can be found in most tropical countries. The lofty, vented roof and open sides provide cooling ventilation. The thatch is watertight and snug, though it must be replaced every few years. In Mexico, simple indigenous pavilions of wood and thatch have existed along the coast for hundreds of years.

Patrician Palapa

The house of Loel Guinness in Acapulco was designed by Guadalajara architect Marco Aldaco. Built in the 1970s on a magnificent hilltop overlooking the bay of Acapulco, the house is a blend of indigenous elements and patrician elegance. Aldaco, who is a Yaqui Indian, designs in a manner resembling a sculptor rather than an architect. After spending time at a site, camping out when necessary, Aldaco becomes familiar with the view, the angles of the sun and the moon, the prevailing breezes, and every detail of the site's topography. Only then is he ready to think about the design. He returns home and waits patiently—and often impatiently—for inspiration to come. When images finally appear in his mind, he records them in quick sketches. It is from these that the final building emerges—working drawings are never used. Aldaco disapproves of T-squares and rulers, feeling that they "belong in the factory." The drawing-up process is carried out, not in an office, but on the site itself—he works with chalk on the ground. Then,

when construction begins, he tells the builders where windows will go, indicating the height with his arms, and working alongside them as the building progresses. This is "hands-on" architecture.

The Guinness house was one of Aldaco's earlier and most successful projects. The owner had a clear vision of what he wanted, and the design was a close collaboration between architect and client. The stucco columns emerged from discussions resulting in a prototype which Aldaco built and showed to Guinness, who then approved it.

The Guinness residence is divided into several separate groups of buildings. Each is more or less invisible from the other, separated by dense tropical foliage, terraces, and winding steps.

OPPOSITE: The swimming pool, behind which is the pavilion housing the study and master bedroom. ABOVE: Simple *equipal* furniture beside the pool.

OVERLEAF: The *palapa*-roofed living area overlooks a paved terrace and the sweep of Acapulco Bay.

CASA
MEXI
CANA
227

Aʙᴏᴠᴇ: A corner of the living room, with traditional Mexican paper flowers. The ceramics are by Gorky. ʀɪɢʜᴛ: The dining room. Shelves on the right are filled with ceramics from Puebla. The floor is covered with a traditional *petate* mat.

Houseguests are an integral pattern of life in Acapulco. In Casa Guinness there is a cottage for guests. This building is set apart from the main house, allowing visitors to be as independent as they wish. The cottage building is placed at the highest level of the site, with its own view over the bay, and a convenient location close to the parking area.

In another building, overlooking the pool and built above a large garage, is Guinness's air-conditioned study. (The air-conditioning is used to combat the devastation which the tropics inflicts on books and papers.) Also in this building is the master bedroom with a verandah.

LEFT, FROM TOP: The living room spreads out below the majestic *palapa* roof. Giant candles, ceramic fruit, and a rustic chair occupy a corner of the dining room. A painted staircase in the garden. OPPOSITE: A ring of stuccoed columns support the main *palapa*, behind which is a natural screen of foliage.

The circular living pavilion forms the third structure, and next to it is a large rectangular dining area. These open onto a landscaped terrace, and each enjoys an eagle's view of the city and bay.

Two Clifftop Houses

Costa Careyes is a private development on a wild and beautiful stretch of coast between Manzanillo and Puerto Vallarta. Created by Gian Franco Brignone, it is managed by his son Giorgio. There is a hotel, a polo club, and a number of houses owned by the Brignone family and their friends. Mexico City-based architect Diego Villaseñor recently built two matching houses side by side on the cliff overlooking the Careyes harbor.

Villaseñor, who has built several other houses in the area, is a little more conventional in his approach to architecture than Aldaco, but his tropical houses share Aldaco's sensuality and careful response to the site. His approach has been to "rescue the way ancient people once lived at the seashore," using the familiar *palapa*. To support these roofs, he brings the jungle right into the house, choosing palms whose trunks have become wrapped by vines.

Architecturally, Villaseñor favors clean, restrained lines, reminiscent of Barragán but

OPPOSITE: Casa Torre and Casa Talec share the same view of the harbor at Costa Careyes. ABOVE: A local cactus has been assimilated into the landscaping of the Casa Torre patio. LEFT: The Casa Torre living room overlooks the pool and harbor and is designed for relaxed living. The "rug" is made of inset black and white beach pebbles.

softened by curved edges. These strong, simple forms offset the ethnic nature of the *palapa* and their supports, resulting in a pavilion form that is primitive, sophisticated, and contemporary, all at once.

The bedrooms are enclosed and are a place of retreat in inclement weather. All sur-

faces, including floors, in these rooms are made of white stucco. Again there are many curves and few hard edges or corners. Windows are open; glass is only used in the bathroom mirrors.

Although the two houses are basically similar, each has distinguishing features. The blue tower in the house owned by Brignone greets visitors as they enter through an outer courtyard. Steps lead up to a tiny, open roof from which one can survey the surrounding landscape. Inside the base of the tower is the TV room.

Visitors to the Casa Talec, the other of the pair, pass through a small, walled patio before entering the main living space. This is punctuated by a central area paved with gray river pebbles resembling a rug. In both houses the *palapa*-covered living area is en-

OPPOSITE: Steps lead from the Casa Torre living area to a pair of guest *palapas*. ABOVE LEFT: A blue tower against a blue sky. Stairs lead up to the roof for sunset watching at Casa Torre. ABOVE: The path from the guest quarters up to the main house at Casa Talec. The timber poles are used as a decorative wall treatment.

tered from the rear at a higher level, allowing the dramatic space within the pavilion and the fabulous view beyond to be revealed simultaneously. In both houses an elegant pool just outside the pavilion seems to hover over the ocean.

ABOVE: A carpet of beach pebbles in the entry patio of Casa Talec. LEFT: The Casa Talec jacuzzi overlooks the harbor. OPPOSITE: The harbor view at Casa Torre is framed by a large Mexican pot and *palapa* fronds.

Santorini in Mexico

Gian Franco Brignone, the founder of Careyes, built a dramatic house for himself on a rocky headland facing away from the harbor. The house feels infinitely more exposed to the ocean and the landscape than the previous houses. Below it is a medley of rocks and islands, surf and surging currents, which has a wildness even on the calmest of days.

The house was designed by Marco Aldaco, and its best feature is a roof terrace reminiscent of the Greek islands, but with a use of color that is unmistakably Mexican.

The terrace is surrounded by a low wall on the ocean side, and has a kitchen and guest rooms at the back. This lofty space seems to be not quite of the earth—floating instead between the sea and the sky.

ABOVE: The roof terrace with simple built-in furniture.
OPPOSITE: The house is built on an exposed rocky headland north of Careyes harbor.

OVERLEAF: The simple horizontal lines of the roof terrace.

Jungle Sanctuary

Zihuatanejo is a small, bustling, and somewhat raffish fishing town set in a sheltered bay on the southern coast of Mexico. Coconut trees line the beaches behind which are steep hills covered in tropical foliage. Separated from the rest of the country by coastal mountains, Zihuatanejo seems divorced from the outside world.

Despite having all the right attributes, Zihuatanejo has miraculously escaped the success syndrome which has converted so many of the world's unspoiled fishing villages into miniature Disneylands.

Among those who have found Zihuatanejo are Jo and Patsy Lo Giudice, and their friends Abby Hoffman, Eleanor and Roland Miller, and artist Larry Rivers. Together they have developed the idyllic retreat shown on these pages.

The house was built some sixteen years ago by former architect and retired art dealer Lo Giudice, who relied less on his architectural training and more on local skills and traditions. The house is a short walk from the popular

OPPOSITE: The bathroom is open to the sky, the birds, the butterflies, and the lizards. TOP: The dining room dresser (found locally) with a colorful assortment of simple ceramics and a painted gourd. ABOVE: The house, with its enveloping thatched roof, is surrounded by tropical vegetation.

Playa de la Ropa, on land that was once a coconut plantation. A primitive brick building, which was originally on the property, has been incorporated into the house. Its roof removed, it has been made into the centrally located master bedroom. Around this are the kitchen, dining room, living room, and additional sleeping areas, all covered by an enveloping roof. There is a lack of outside walls—as is often seen in the tropics—resulting in uninterrupted views of a garden lushly furnished with orchids, bougainvillea, hyacinth, and hibiscus.

The roof is thatched, and it is designed to withstand typhoons. The local palm thatch is distributed in dense layers providing excellent insulation: the bleached surface facing the sky has good reflective properties, and the myriad airpockets within prevent the transmission of heat. The structure is a local rough-out hardwood that still looks as good as new, and is so hard that nails could not penetrate it unless holes were predrilled. Lo Giudice covered the brick walls of the master bedroom with an improvised plaster mix of clay, cement, and aniline dyes.

Over the years the house has grown more civilized. The original sand floor has been covered with local *bara* tiles, overlaid with Berber rugs. Both new and antique furniture has been added from local sources. The Lo Giudices, who own a popular restaurant in town called Coconuts, usually spend up to six months a year in the house, and so it needs to function as more than an occasional vacation home. The climate of course takes its toll on furnishings. Books, for example, cannot be expected to withstand more than four years of the intense humidity.

A succession of visitors come and go, particularly during the winter season. The house's original intended role as a kind of seasonal salon for artists and writers has been fulfilled.

CASA
MEXI
CANA
247

The living room, open to the elements, has an uninterrupted view of a garden furnished with orchids, bougainvillea, and hibiscus. The distinctive wooden rocking chair is of local design.

CHAPTER NINE

THE MEXICAN INFLUENCE

T hanks to an ever-expanding Hispanic population, the southwestern part of the United States is becoming increasingly aware of the culture of Mexico. Nowhere is this more apparent than in Los Angeles, where storefronts and billboards in certain parts of the city are entirely in Spanish, reminding its residents that Los Angeles grew originally from a tiny *pueblo* on land that was, until the middle of the last century, a part of Mexico itself.

The architectural styles of many Los Angeles houses readily show the influence of Mexico. The Spanish colonial bungalow usually featured a variety of detailing (niches, arched openings, and decorative tilework) in the Mexican colonial idiom. And the ubiquitous ranch-style houses pioneered by architect Cliff May (himself a descendant of the early Spanish settlers in southern California) evolved from the early Mexican *ranchos* in which his ancestors lived.

The Mexican influence, however, embraces both architecture and decoration. Often artists are the first to react to changes in their visual environment, and the increasing presence of Mexican culture in Los Angeles has drawn a response from a group of resident artists and designers. This group was aware of the colors and shapes of Barragán, but the major influence was Frida Kahlo's house.

The proximity of Baja California has also proved to be an inspirational catalyst. The visual impact of Tijuana seen from the 405 Freeway while traveling from San Diego is one of unexpected color; the hillsides are dotted in a mosaic of vividly colored houses.

O PPOSITE: A corner of landscape designer Nancy Power's terrace in Santa Monica, California. An opening in the stuccoed wall reveals a small sunken garden. The brightly painted edging was inspired by wall treatments seen in Mexico.

249

Melrose Casita

Hilary and Michael Anderson have transformed their typical 1920s Mediterranean-style cottage in Hollywood into a Mexican cottage. The Andersons are British clothes designers with their own retail store, Clacton and Frinton, on La Cienega Boulevard in Los Angeles. Their house is on a quiet street only a block away from the busiest section of Melrose Avenue.

The entrance is landscaped with tropical plants, and Michael Anderson, who trained as a graphic artist, painted the inside of the house with bands of color recalling interiors in Oaxaca. The lower part of the walls in the living room are painted blue, above which is a hand-painted frieze; the underside of the arches is a soft turquoise. These colors were sanded back to give them an authentic, faded Mexican patina. Wooden windows and doors are turquoise on the outside, white on the inside. Some of the furniture, covered with Guatemalan fabrics, was handpainted by Michael Anderson.

Much of the Andersons' time at home is spent on their loggia. This faces a large back garden, which is planted with tropical foliage and palm trees and is where the Andersons eat and entertain, while

Aʙᴏᴠᴇ: The Andersons' loggia faces the back garden and is the center of family activity. ʟᴇғᴛ: In the dining room a simple, painted chair blends with Michael Anderson's hand-painted frieze and wall treatment. ᴏᴘᴘᴏsɪᴛᴇ: The brightly painted kitchen opens into a sunny breakfast room.

LEFT: An outdoor playhouse, with miniature Mexican chairs, was painted to match the patio colors. BELOW LEFT: A view from the sitting room toward the dining room and kitchen. The painted-wood lamp is by artist Paul Glynn, who lives and works in Guatemala. RIGHT: The fireplace, decorated with a variety of artifacts from Mexico and elsewhere. The frieze was painted by Michael Anderson.

their children play on swings suspended from overhead beams. The loggia walls are painted the same blue as the interior, and the windows are framed by a broad painted band of terra cotta.

The Mexican theme of the Andersons' house evolved naturally from their affinity with Mexico. The bright colors have also produced a cheerful environment for their children.

Memphis Fiesta

Peter Shire is an American artist and a member of Milan's Memphis group. He was born and raised in the predominantly Mexican neighborhood of Echo Park, near downtown Los Angeles, and this influence shows itself primarily in the bright, uninhibited colors of his ceramics and recent metal sculptures. But it is also seen in the façades and interiors of his houses.

Shire recently moved across the street from his sculptural, highly colored earlier house which resembled one of his famous teapots. His new house, like the previous one, is basically a simple 1940s tract house, and is still in the process of being adapted to the Shire aesthetic. People who do not know Shire always assume that the two houses are owned by particularly extravert Mexicans.

LEFT: A corner of the Shire sitting room. BELOW: Shire's vividly colored deck, recently built, is raised treetop-high above his garden in Echo Park, a Mexican neighborhood that has influenced his work and his home designing.

ABOVE: The newly painted side elevation of his earlier house (now passed on to his brother, Billy), seen from the porch of his new house. RIGHT: The bedroom, with a Shire-designed cabinet.

Hillside Retreat

British-born graphic designer Mick Haggerty has lived in Los Angeles since 1973. Initially attracted to the city by the graphic qualities of its visual environment, he has frequently used elements of its urban landscape in his work.

In recent years he has explored the Baja peninsula on fishing trips with friends. Attracted by the uninhibited combinations of bright colors used on the front surfaces of houses in northern Mexico, he bought a range of colors at a Tijuana paint store. He began applying these to his one-story cottage in the Hollywood Hills, transforming its ubiquitous 1950s façade.

Haggerty also opened up the interior of the house, which he describes as being a "dark and pokey hole" when he bought it; it is now pared down to the basic elements of its original architecture. Walls have been removed, and its minimal elegance combines with vibrant Mexican colors to give it a sunny ambience.

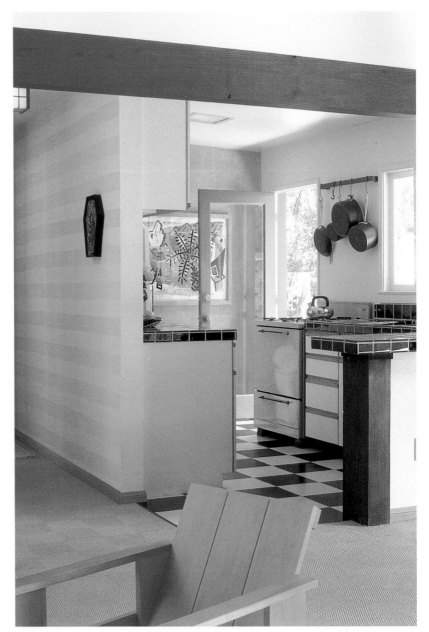

ABOVE: Haggerty opened up the space between the living room and kitchen. Stripes line the passage at left. OPPOSITE: A Haggerty painting of the coast of Baja California gives a sunny, graphic focus to a simple kitchen.

OPPOSITE: Inspired by colorful house fronts in Ensenada, Haggerty filled his car with Mexican house paint and transformed his 1950s Hollywood Hills cottage, inside and out. The curtains and bedcover delicately complete the transformation. ABOVE: The patio deck, with multi-colored breakfast table. LEFT: The terrace, which faces a view of a small canyon.

Artist's Villa

This 1920s Mediterranean-style house in the Hollywood Hills had fallen victim to a failed attempt at conversion to a 1950s tract house when Anne Kelly, an artist from Australia, found it.

In the process of restoring the house to the builder's original intention, she has given it a distinctively Mexican character, inspired by the early California missions and her many trips to Mexico.

Kelly began by using color to link the rooms, emulating both the fresh and faded paint of old Mexican walls. Friezes tied the open-plan rooms together, giving the central dining room the feel of a courtyard. Themes as well as colors reappear: a zigzag skirt on a table links up with the top of a nearby screen, and blues and yellows reappear in various shades and textures throughout the house.

The roof terrace was added to give character and shade to the house. Designed by the architects Batey and Mack, it was built with old handmade roof tile, found in salvage yards, as it was important that the terrace appear part of the original house.

The upstairs rooms are small, and Kelly furnished them to look like a Mexican cottage. She found Mexican campesino furniture for several of the rooms and used woven cotton blankets found in the craft markets of Mexico City as curtains. In the spirit of Frida Kahlo, Kelly has collected many *retablos* and *ex-votos*, with their potential to refuel an artist's imagination.

Kelly exhibits regularly as a functional artist, and the

OPPOSITE: The dining room is framed by chintz curtains with a Barbarian chair by Garouste & Bonetti in the foreground. The dining table was designed and built by Annie Kelly, who also painted the walls. ABOVE: The chairs and dresser were found in Arte de Mexico, a store in North Hollywood. The *retablo* (tin painting), pottery, and other artifacts were found on trips to Mexico. In the foreground is a ubiquitous *equipal* table.

house provides a showcase for her work and the furniture of other artists—including Jon Bok, Peter Shire, Jim Ganzer, Paul Glynn, Phil Garner, and Andrew Logan—with whom she has shown.

Each of her visits to Mexico has meant more additions to the growing collection of indigenous arts and crafts in the house.

Paved with Mexican tile, the roof terrace was designed by architects Batey and Mack. The roof tiles were recycled from a demolition site to maintain the period character of the house.

LEFT: The dining room, with a Kelly-designed table and a chest of drawers by Jon Bok. BELOW: Open shelves, filled with Mexican pottery, in the kitchen. The chair is from Arte de Mexico.

ABOVE: A corner of the dining room with a frieze and wall treatment by Kelly. RIGHT: A Mexican corner table from the Luz de Jesus store in Hollywood, with cocktails, and pottery by Clarice Cliff in Mexican colors.

Hubcap Hacienda

Jon Bok is a young artist from the Midwest. He now shares a house near Melrose Avenue with Robert Lopez, the curator of the Luz de Jesus gallery on Melrose Avenue, which shows the work of Hispanic-influenced artists. Lopez has recently achieved a certain notoriety locally with his stage appearances as El Vez, the Mexican Elvis, which is a Lopez-created parody of Elvis impersonators. (In his stage performances he claims to be the illegitimate son of Elvis Presley and Charo.)

Jon Bok successfully blends Mexican and primitive American influences in his folk-art furniture, which is embellished with bottle caps and other recycled materials. His house is decorated with this furniture, which is steadily replaced as it sells, and with a rich blend of Mexican and Guatemalan folk art.

One wall of the living room is covered with hubcaps collected from the streets of Los Angeles (Bok's previous house was dramatically decorated with hubcaps hung on the outside walls, illuminated at night with colored spot-

lights), and the adjacent wall is hung with part of their collection of anonymous paintings found in thrift stores. The passage wall leading to the bedroom is covered with rows and rows of Mexican masks used for the Day of the Dead, an important festival in Mexico celebrated at the end of October.

Bok's ability to make a powerful graphic statement from found materials of this kind is a gift which he shares with folk artists everywhere.

A BOVE: The exterior at twilight, illuminated by colored patio lights. RIGHT: An altar-like table in the living room, on which there are several of Bok's wooden crosses. The primitive wooden bust is from Guatemala.

O VERLEAF: The hubcap theme is continued in the living room, with furniture by Bok, a traditional Mexican Day of the Dead skeleton figure, and decorated Day of the Dead masks.

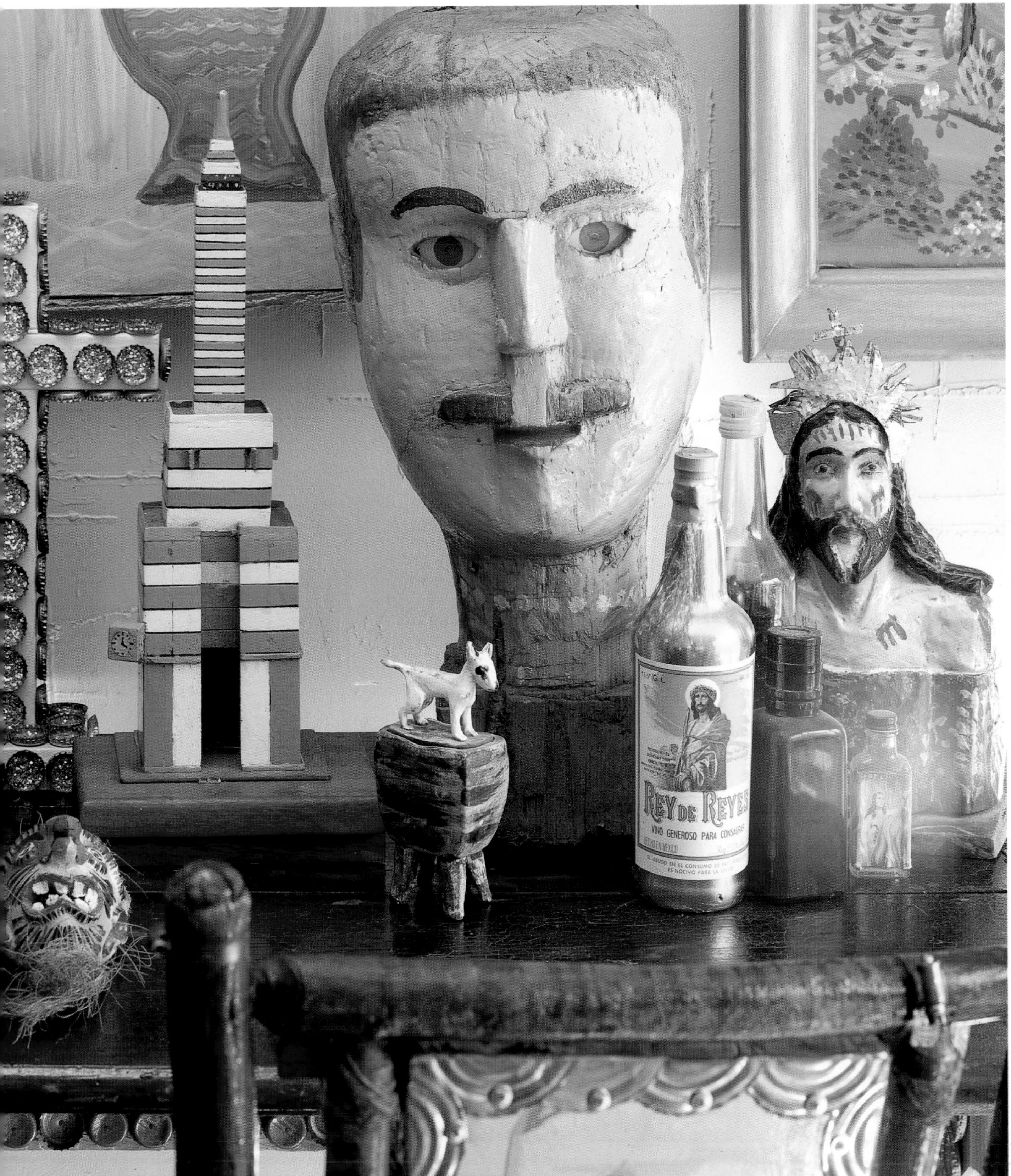
REY DE REYES
VINO GENEROSO PARA CONSAGRA

ABOVE: The fireplace is surrounded by Mexican artifacts and Bok-designed furniture. LEFT: A well-populated corner of the living room, with more Bok furniture. Sitting in the studded armchair is a *campesino* figure from Guatemala. OPPOSITE: The breakfast nook is delineated by more hubcaps; the chair is another Bok design.

Index

270

CASA
MEXI
CANA
271

Acknowledgments

Even though she was busy with her own work during the production of this book, the artist Annie Kelly was, as always, my major inspiration.

My deepest gratitude to Marie-Pierre Colle, who found most of the Mexican locations, coordinated the photography, and provided endless hospitality. Thanks to her matchless professional and personal contacts all the best doors were opened, and because of her enthusiasm and love of her country the task of completing the photography in Mexico could not have been more pleasurable or fulfilling.

The architect Manolo Mestre was influential in the development of the book and gave generously of his time and knowledge, especially the week we spent on the road documenting the chapter on primitive houses and parts of the hacienda chapter.

Thanks also to architect Enrique Norten for his hospitality, advice, and friendship. A house of his which I had hoped to include in the book was sadly not ready in time.

I am also grateful to Erendira de la Lama for her assistance with houses and the former convents in Puebla, and to Fernando González Gortázar, for his similar help with access to early Barragán houses in Guadalajara.

Others who gave advice and help include Lily Kassner, Dr. Sabino Yano, Cristina Galvez, Eric Gibeler, Ted Guefen, Esperanza de Haro, Fernando and Rosalba Ortiz Monasterio, Antonio Enriquez Savignac (Minister of Tourism), and Lic. Javier Rivas from the Office of Tourism.

Needless to say I am grateful to all the architects and homeowners who allowed us to photograph and were so kind and hospitable, always with the spirit of *mi casa es su casa*.

The book was conceived in the house of our friends, Larry Williams and Leslie Libman (a corner of which is shown on this page) when, after many shared adventures in Baja California and Oaxaca, and with a mutual love of all things Mexican, someone said, "Why not do a Mexico book?"

Metropolitan Home very kindly allowed us to use photographs of the houses of Mick Haggerty and Peter Shire; *House Beautiful*, the patio of Nancy Power; and *HG*, some photographs of Casa Torre in Careyes.

My final thanks go to my editor, Roy Finamore, who is the best!

Designed by Joseph Rutt

Composed in Memphis Medium and Futura Book by Trufont Typographers, Inc., Hicksville, New York

Printed and bound by Toppan Printing Company, Ltd., Tokyo, Japan